Two Ways Out

Two Ways Out

*A Story of God's Unfailing
and Redemptive Love*

MELVIN AND JENNIFER RANKINS

Two Ways Out
by Melvin and Jennifer Rankins

Cover Design by Atinad Designs.

© Copyright 2014

SAINT PAUL PRESS, DALLAS, TEXAS, First Printing, 2014

This is a work of fiction. Names, characters, places and incidents
either are products of the author's imagination or are used
fictitiously. Any resemblance to actual events or locales or persons,
living or dead, is entirely coincidental.

ISBN-10: 0-9915856-7-4
ISBN-13: 978-0-9915856-7-0

Printed in the U.S.A.

"Moreover, the Lord said unto me, Take thee a great scroll and write in it with an ordinary pen."

ISAIAH 8:1

Introduction

What! You wrote a book about a PROSTITUTE? Yes. She is actually a harlot named Gomer who continued to run from her husband and into the world while her faithful husband, Hosea, would go after her as God had instructed him. But don't worry; we've cleaned it up as much as we could, considering this is a story from the Bible. Now, sit back and enjoy as you read about God's unfailing love and redemption for the Prophet Hosea and his promiscuous bride, Gomer. **Reader's discretion is advised.**

Background

Hosea was directed by God to marry a promiscuous woman (or prostitute) named Gomer, and he did so. Marriage, here, is symbolic of the covenantal relationship between God and Israel. However, Israel has been unfaithful to God by following other gods and breaking the commandments which are the terms of the covenant, hence, Israel is symbolized by a harlot who violates the obligations of marriage to her husband. In Hosea 3:1-3, Hosea is commanded to go back and love Gomer. He buys Gomer back with fifteen shekels.

Gomer kept wandering into the arms of other lovers. She was unfaithful; yet the Lord told Hosea to keep going after her again and again, and bring her back home.

Hosea was a picture of God and Gomer represented God's

people. God's people were called to live in a covenant relationship with the Lord. He was their God and they were to have no other gods in their life. They consistently rebelled against God, though, and chased after idols. Their history was full of sin and unfaithfulness.

God uses this peculiar story to illustrate the unfailing love He has for His people. They, like Gomer, had turned their backs on God. They, like Gomer, proved themselves unfaithful to their commitment to God. With indifference and willful intention, they resumed their old lifestyle, which did not honor God or obey His laws.

Hosea mirrors the constancy of God's love. He says in Hosea 14:4: "I will heal their backsliding. I will love them freely." Did Gomer deserve that kind of forgiveness? Do we deserve that kind of forgiveness? God's love extends beyond the limits of our sinful humanity. He longs to draw us into a state of restoration with Himself. However merciful God is, He adds this crucial condition to His mercy as recorded in Hosea 5:15: "I will return again to my place till they acknowledge their offense."

Acknowledgements

To the reader, we say thank you for purchasing this book. This story is guaranteed to reach both the head and the heart. It is one of the greatest pictures of God's love and faithfulness found throughout the Bible. The truth is, we are a bunch of Gomers who chase after the world. And yet our God has a love greater than that of Hosea and will pursue us and bring us back to Himself.

We would like to thank a few people for their extraordinary help and contribution to this worthy project. First of all, we thank God for His faithfulness towards us, His loving kindness towards us, and His new mercies we see day after day.

Also, we would like to give a huge shout out to our good friend, Rachel Ketring, for helping out with a few additional details to make Gomer's life more interesting. Thank you so much, Rachel.

A special thank you to our readers. It is you we have in mind when we're staring at the computer and creating characters such as Hilton and Grace, characters who can be a representation of any one of us.

And finally, a big thanks to our publisher, St. Paul Press, and editors at Fresh Eyes. You guys are the best of the best.

—————

As husband and wife, this is our second literary offering together. We are so excited that you (the reader) continue to support our work and believe in us. Our prayer is that you will be inspired by this riveting love story. So, sit back as you journey along with our characters (Hosea, aka, **Hilton**, and Gomer, aka, **Grace**) and discover God's redemptive love and faithfulness toward His people.

This book is dedicated to all the Hoseas and Gomers out there. You know who you are!

Preface

This story is a work of fiction inspired by the redemptive love of God from the Holy Bible—the Book of Hosea. This story is based on the Prophet Hosea and his wife, Gomer. Hosea was an Old Testament prophet who God used in a very unique way. Not only did Hosea speak the words of God, but God turned his life and marriage into a living parable for the people of God to see and witness everywhere.

This is not the only story in the Bible about a harlot. In the book of Matthew, we take a look at the lineage of Christ: Rahab was a prostitute, yet she hid the spies and kept them safe; Bathsheba had an adulterous affair with King David, and when she found out she was pregnant by him, her lover plotted the murder of her husband to hide their affair and the baby.

Jesus accepted the woman at the well who can only be deemed as a scandalous woman as she had had five husbands; but He followed His acceptance by challenging her directly about her promiscuity. Jesus also stopped the stoning of another woman caught in the act of adultery, and made it clear He was not going to condemn her, but then pointedly admonished her to turn from her adulterous ways. So, as we can see from all of these accounts from the Bible, **grace** flowed freely from Jesus in a way that can only be because He loves us.

AUTHORS' NOTE:

Apart from Biblical references to our characters, any event or locations used in the depiction of this story of Hosea should not be construed as real, but rather fictional; they're a product of our imagination. Any personal resemblance to people—living or dead—is solely coincidental.

Chapter One

— *et* —

"Raise your glass, everyone. Let's celebrate to our life!
To our love," Hilton said as everyone around the table raised
their glasses high.

"Cheers! Let's make a toast to all the years we've been
married," Grace said as a single tear escaped from the corner
of her eye. It was their wedding anniversary, a day they had
both looked forward to celebrating with good friends.

They'd been married now for fifteen years, but things
were not always roses between them. They had their good
days, good weeks, good months, even good years. However,
Hilton never knew what triggered his wife to cause her to go
back out into the world, a world he knew little about except
for those times he had to go out and find her amongst the
wolves somewhere in the city of Cleveland. That's when he'd
discovered just how dangerous it was out there.

It was a world filled with men and women who had a
strange hold on his wife. Maybe she liked the attention. Maybe
she liked her freedom. He just wished he knew what it was

about being out there that always beckoned her back into that life style. He often prayed and asked God how many times would he have to put up with this going back and forth? Yet, God always prompted him once again to go out there and find her, and bring her home to himself and to their three boys.

But he didn't want to think about that today. No. Not today. Today was their wedding anniversary and he'd planned on making it a good day. They were celebrating along with a few friends who had stopped over and who wanted to extend their congratulations to the couple. Shane and Christi had known Hilton and Grace since high school. They all went to prom and got married about the same time, had children the same age, and exchanged gifts every year at Christmas. They had even gone on a few vacations together.

It wasn't until after Hilton and Grace had their third child, when Grace surprised everyone with an announcement that she wanted to join a health club and take strength training classes three days a week. Hilton did not see the need for her to join a health club as she was already as skinny as a bean pole. Her young, beautiful, and flawless face housed eyes the color of which she could change by wearing amber contact lenses. Grace had long jet-black hair and always pulled it back into a ponytail. She was just the right height and had the beauty to pass for a model on any runway. However, something was stirring inside of her, and nothing seemed to satisfy her until she was back out there amongst the wolves.

"My beautiful wife," Hilton said. "Let me wipe away your tears. What are you crying for? Don't you know by now how much I love you and I forgave you for what has happened in the past?" Hilton stood up and took his wife by the hand and pulled her up closer to him. "Honey, let's put the past behind us and make this evening a special celebration." Hilton turned to their friends and smiled, but he could see how uncomfortable they were around Grace when she got like this.

Shane and Christi had three boys also, and a fourth child on the way, which was exciting news because it was their first girl. They were counting down the days to delivering their little bundle of joy. They lived in a new development in the heights where all the neighbors were close and bonded like family.

"Actually, we can't stay long, guys. We just wanted to stop by and have a toast with you guys and drop off your anniversary gift," Christi said. "I hope you like it." Hilton had placed the gift on the kitchen table when they first arrived. It was gift wrapped so beautifully, and Grace had refused to open it while they were there. But then again, she always waited until her guests left before she would open any gift from anyone.

Hilton went along with the idea that Grace was too shy and embarrassed to open gifts in front of others. However, the real truth was, Grace didn't feel as if she deserved a gift from anyone. She didn't deserve these two best friends who had stood by her side through thick and thin, even helping Hilton out with the boys while she was off on one of her escapades, sometimes for months at a time. But it never stopped her from going. In some strange way, she looked forward to creating more chaos.

"We better get going," Christi said. "It's getting late and our neighbor has the boys." Shane knew it was about time to leave also. Something just wasn't right with Grace tonight. "Yeah, and Christi needs to get off her feet and rest," Shane added before getting up as he extended his hands to his wife to help lift her from the dining room chair.

"Well, if you insist on leaving, but we'd love to have you stay for dinner," Hilton said trying to sound convincing. "I made a big pot of my famous shrimp pasta dish that you guys love. We have plenty of garlic bread and salad to go around. Plus, our kids are staying overnight at their grandmother's, so…"

"No. No." Shane interrupted. "But, thanks so much. We need to get going." Shane and Christi both hugged and kissed Hilton and Grace before walking towards the front door. After another round of good byes, Grace finally slumped down into the couch in front of the entertainment center like a deflated balloon.

"What's wrong, honey. Do you want me to fix your plate now?"

"No. I'm not really hungry," Grace said as she poured herself another glass of champagne.

"Well, would you like to watch a movie or something? We have a bunch of movies in that stack over there—never seen before," he said pointing to the stack.

"No, Hilton. I do not want to watch a movie, either!" Hilton saw the agitation on her face and heard it in her voice; he had no clue what was provoking her sudden mood change.

"Well, how about we watch a program on TV. Maybe HBO has something worthwhile showing?" he tried again.

"Hilton, for crying out loud, I do not want to watch TV! I do not want to do anything. As a matter of fact, I need some air." She jumped up from the couch, spilling her drink down the front of her blouse.

"I'm sorry!" Hilton said. "Can't you see that I am trying? This is not easy for me, but as I promised you, I will do whatever it takes to make you happy here at home. So, you tell me, what do *you* want to do?"

"Hilton, please stop patronizing me. I told you what happened will never happen again. As for that man you met in the bar, he was just a friend. Nothing happened."

She saw the anguish in his face. "Hilton, I wish I was more like you. I feel as though I've ruined your life. I just wish I believed like you believe, Hilton. I get easily complicit and antsy and I cannot stand these four walls when I get like this. They close in on me and I feel smothered." She looked at him for some sign that he understood her words, but it was useless.

"But, I'm home now and things are going to be different. Just be patient with me. I'll prove my love to you and our children," Grace continued.

Grace stood up to walk out for some fresh air spilling the half empty bottle of champagne on to the white carpet. "Oh, my God, now look what you made me do!" Instead of running for a paper towel, Hilton stood there amazed at how fast the liquid soaked into the fabric and how Grace had that familiar blank stare in her eyes. He knew that look quite well as he'd seen it way too often.

He finally moved his feet and ran into the kitchen where he grabbed the roll of paper towels and pressed a huge handful into the carpet to soak up the spilled champagne. This just made Grace more agitated with Hilton. She knew he had walked around on egg shells for the whole twelve months since she'd been back home. He'd catered to her every need, trying to please her, doing everything to try to make her want to be home with him and the boys.

But it didn't last long. Grace seemed to have a built-in timer inside her. Only, this time, Hilton was going to fight harder to not let her leave. He had made all those inner vows that if he ever got her home this last time, she was not leaving to go back out there again. But, he was wrong.

Grace had to fight hard to stay. It was so much easier to be back out there where she thought she belonged—a stronghold that would not let go of her—and Hilton saw it in her eyes. *"Lord, I love her, but it's always going to be like this with her, isn't it?"*

Chapter Two

————— *et* —————

The following evening things started to escalate. He followed Grace from room to room as they argued. Finally, following her into the bedroom, Hilton was at his wit's end with trying to convince her that this is where she needed to be—home with him and their three kids.

"Grace, you're always on me to keep pressing toward the higher mark. You tell me to be strong. You encourage me to step up to the plate, to be a man. Yet, you constantly run away from me, Grace. How much more can one man take?" Hilton was angry as he watched his wife stuff her garments into an overnight bag. He wondered why she even packed a bag at all. The items she took with her never came back home. It always ended the same way. By the time he found her (either working as a barmaid or dancing), she would have lost all her things and would be surviving on the money from the night clubs.

Now it began to make sense to him why she suddenly wanted to take up strength training at the gym. One of her friends, another dancer, had told Grace it would help her to become "*fluid*" while dancing on the pole. How many times in the past had he found her in a night club as she walked off stage and into a dressing room; he'd sneak in and demanded she come home with him. How many times had he shoved pictures of the boys in her face to convince her to walk away from that life and to come back home with him? But it was becoming harder and harder.

"Grace, are you even listening to me? I'm only human. How can you keep doing this to us?" Hilton demanded. "You keep telling me you're trying to change, and how you're never going back out there. Do you remember the last time how you promised me never to do this again?"

Tears were streaming down Grace's face, but it didn't stop her from packing her things. "Look, I don't want to hear this right now. I just need to get away for a while and think things through."

"But, Grace. How can you, after all we've been through?" Hilton sat on the edge of the bed and held his head in his hands. His face was wet with tears. He had prayed for his family every day and begged God to intervene on behalf of his wife. He didn't understand why this was happening. Was God trying to teach him a lesson? And what about their kids? Did she even care? No. How could she? "Grace, what am I supposed to do now?"

"Look, Hilton, it's just the way it is. I just need to get away for a while. It's just too much stress for me right now. I will call you later and we'll talk."

"Stress! Really, Grace? You have no idea what stress is about. After you walk out of that door, I will have to go to your mother's house, pick up the kids and explain to them that their mother is gone—again. How am I supposed to explain that to them or to your mother for God's sake?"

"Just, tell them I'll be back soon. I'm sorry, but I must go now."

Hilton followed his wife through the house into the living room where he noticed their drinking glasses from the night before. He was willing to try anything to keep his wife from leaving. He always reverted to becoming a desperate man when she got like this. He'd do anything—anything—to keep his wife from leaving.

He ran over and picked up one of the glasses. "Please, my beautiful wife," he said through tears. "Please stay here with me. Wipe away your tears and let us celebrate." He quickly grabbed the empty bottle of champagne and tried to shove it into her hand. "Raise your glasses everybody," he said. "Cheers! Let's toast to all these years."

But, Grace quickly turned away and kept walking. She threw her bag into the back seat of her car and quickly slammed the door. Before Hilton could reason with her any further, she pulled out of the driveway and within seconds she was gone.

Hilton watched as the car turned the corner and was out of sight. Could Grace survive all the sharks who'd be circling around her when she arrived in the city? She was beautiful, graceful, and walked with a confidence like nobody else he had ever met. She was royalty to him—a major catch—pure beauty. Even though it was hard to convince Grace of her beauty, he knew she would be vulnerable to any stranger out there. She had been in the past.

———————

It was after ten o'clock that night when Grace pulled into the parking lot of Ace's Night Club. She sat in her car for a long time before mustering enough courage to walk into the club near downtown Cleveland in the heart of the theater district. She knew a few of the girls from when she'd worked there before. It felt like ages ago but had only been a little over a year.

Her friend, Maxi, had gotten her in as a pole dancer at Ace's, but the owner at that time, Anthony, had taken one look at her and said, "With your pure beauty and a body like that, you should seriously consider doing more than just dancing, if you know what I mean." She thought about it for a second, but then said, "Nope," in her defiant voice. "That is not an option so don't even go there!"

Back then Maxi and Grace were dancing three times a week and making a lot of money. That was before Hilton and his brother had barged into the place one night before closing and pulled her out of the back room forcing her into his car. The security guards were furious. But, there wasn't anything they or Anthony could do once they found out she was legally married to this man.

Grace was glad when Hilton had come looking for her to get her out of there. She was getting tired of Anthony pressing her about taking her skills to another level in the hotel across the street. He'd told her he had men lined up to pay her big bucks for a half hour of her time. But, for some reason she just couldn't do it, although she realized later it must have been her husband's prayers for protection all along. She thought that was the last time she'd ever see her friend Maxi again. So when she walked into the night club and headed straight for the bar, Maxi thought she was seeing a ghost.

"Grace! Oh, my God. I thought I'd never see you again." They bear-hugged before Maxi pulled her back as they rocked back and forth, and she inspected Grace like she was a specimen. "Girl, you look fabulous! What have you been up to? We missed you."

Maxi led her over to the bar and ordered two Cosmopolitans as they caught up on life. "Girl, I had no idea you were married and had three children? Oh, my God, Grace. How could you be here, knowing they're three hours away from you? And, that was your husband who came in here last time and took you home?" It wasn't a question, more like a statement. Maxi just couldn't imagine leaving her kids or wrap her mind around the fact that Grace was a married woman while she danced for Ace's Lounge and had never said a word.

Maxi, herself, was single with no children. "So, have you gotten yourself hitched up yet?" Grace asked while sipping on her drink.

"Well, I guess if Mr. Right came along, I would definitely know it and if he matched my must have list, I would be out of here so fast." Maxi started going down her imaginary 'must have' list: "must be good looking, must own his own home, must drive a big fancy car, must pay for a huge wedding and big reception, then we'd settle down, have two kids, a dog, a cat, a gated privacy fence around it with a pool, and oh, don't forget we will go to Disney every year for vacation."

"Yeah, yeah! We all say that in the beginning," Grace said in her 'just kidding' tone. "But keep on dreaming, girl. And someday Mr. Right is going to walk right in those doors..." (Grace pointed to the gold-plated double doors at the entrance.) "And he will sweep you right off your feet. So, keep on dreaming, girl." They both burst out laughing.

Maxi did dream of Mr. Right walking through those doors someday, but until then, she was planning to dance her way to the top and through college and become a registered nurse. Saving her money and living her life to the fullest, she had long since given up her dreams of ever following in her mother's path and someday becoming a best selling author. Her mother was the famous Lillian Turner who had written a series of murder and suspense books about Hilton Head Island. Her mom traveled and did book signings all over the world. That was not Maxi's cup of tea. Like Grace, she loved to dance.

"So, where is Ant?" Grace asked as she scanned the dark room. "Is he hiding in the back with his girls, or out taking care of business?"

"Neither!" Maxi said. "Actually Anthony is no longer the owner of Ace's Lounge. Not long after you left Ant sold the club and left town. We're under a new owner named Levi now. But, I'm telling you right now, he's nothing like Anthony. This guy is a lot harder to work for and tighter with his money; won't give us any overtime no matter how much money we bring in for him. He runs a tight ship. I'll go get him and introduce you if you're thinking about coming back."

Grace had to think about it for a minute. Anthony had always been generous with his money. The girls worked overtime, but if they needed a day off here and there, he was always accommodating. Ant never pressured them, and always provided security while they were on stage and in the back. And when they left the bar at closing he had someone to escort them out to the parking lot. She wondered if this guy was anything like that. After a few minutes she would find out. She finished her drink and turned to Maxi. "Yeah, I guess it'll be okay. I'll go meet him."

"Great. And, welcome back. Now remember, Levi is going to want to interview you like you're fresh off the street since he knows nothing about you. So, don't get upset when he asks you to audition for him."

Audition for him! Grace thought about her statement. She was not going to audition for anybody. She knew she had the stuff it took to work at any club. Ace's Lounge was not her only choice.

"Girl, how long has it been?" Maxi asked.

"I don't know! I guess I've been gone from this scene for about a year; but this is the longest time I've ever stayed away. But you know me. I couldn't take those four walls anymore. Had to come back."

"Back to what, Grace?" Maxi asked sounding perplexed. "Girl, this is no life. You have three small children at home. Why would you want to come back to this?"

"Don't know. I just do. Okay. I can't explain it so stop pressing me." Maxi shrugged her shoulders. She could never understand girls like Grace. In her eyes, Grace had it all. A beautiful home, a faithful husband, beautiful children, and according to Grace, Hilton provided a nice income so she didn't need to work at all; she was even a stay-at-home mom. She could only dream of having that life someday.

"Suit yourself. Follow me." They walked toward the back of the lounge where the doors were always closed and all the secrets were kept. For some reason, Grace felt nervous for the first time. She always blamed Hilton when she felt like this. He was always on his knees praying and asking God to intervene in her life, putting a stop to whatever it was that kept pulling her back out into the world; and on many occasions she felt like his God was protecting her from harm.

This was one of those times she knew he must have been praying. She swallowed, then took in a deep breath and stood firm as Maxi knocked on the blood red door.

Chapter Three

―――――― *et* ――――――

"Come on in," he said in his Berry White baritone voice. Grace felt intimidated right off the bat. "And, who is this, Maxi?"

"This is my friend, Grace. She used to work here back when Ant was running the club. Grace, this is Levi." All of a sudden Grace felt like a teenager. What had happened to all that confidence? A bead of sweat popped out on her forehead as he extended his hand.

"Nice to meet you, Grace. Are you here looking to get your job back?" She noticed two other men standing in the room. Why she hadn't noticed them when she walked into the room was beyond her, but they inspected her up and down like she was a piece of meat.

"Yes, I am, Sir. I meant, yes, I am looking to getting my job back." She switched legs as she shifted from one foot to the other. Then she decided to put one hand on her hip and show this man she meant business, not that it made a difference with him.

"So, were you one of the bar maids?" Levi lit up one of those funny looking cigarettes that was laced with drugs. She could smell it. He took in a deep drag and blew it out in her direction sending smoke all over her. It was like she'd been engulfed in a cloud. The scent assaulted her nose, but she was not backing down.

"No. I was a dancer just like Maxi here." She looked over at Maxi who was preoccupied with one of the guys standing in the room. He had his hands all over her. She let out a giggle or two, but Grace knew from working there before, Maxi did not fool around with any of these guys and especially the ones employed by the owner. She was probably just letting them get their kicks on while she vouched for her dancing skills.

All of a sudden Levi sat upright in his tall swivel chair and stared at Grace. "How old are you may I ask?"

"Twenty-nine. I'll be thirty in a few months."

He stared at her in silence then leaned back in his chair again.

"Stop joking with me. What is your real age?"

Grace was not expecting a challenge, although Maxi was much younger than she was. But still, she had her by at least three years.

"Twenty-nine." She reached into her purse and pulled out her driver's license.

Levi held it out in his hand and slowly got up and walked around the desk. He stared at her for a few more seconds. His eyes bore though her as though he could see all her secrets, and then he inspected the ID again.

"This could be a fake."

"Yes, and it could be real too," she snapped back at him.

"When was the last time you danced?"

"Twelve months ago when I last worked here."

"And, why did you quit, or did you get fired?"

"Fired? No. I didn't get fired. And, I didn't quit either. I had a family emergency and had to leave immediately. It's taken me awhile to get back to where I was." She was not going to explain to this man or anybody else for that matter why her husband could suddenly show up unannounced and drag her out, sometimes kicking and screaming, so that he had to, at times, literally tie her down before he could drive off the lot.

He stared at her again as if he didn't believe a word she was telling him.

"So, show me?"

"Show you what?"

"That you can dance."

"Right now?"

He nods his head up and down.

"But, there's no music."

"So?"

He gets up and goes over to a stereo system and pushes some buttons. Suddenly the music begins to play. Her instincts tell her to back away, but she wanted this job. No, she needed this job, and this need was not foreign to Grace. She's tried to figure out where this was coming from. But when she tried to stop it, she was unhappy and discontented.

The music begins to play, but Grace was not going to let him get under her skin. She wasn't a beginner dancer, and she certainly was not going to dance for him right here and now with his two cronies watching and gawking. After he saw she was not moving, he hit the off button and walked back behind his desk.

"Mondays, Wednesdays, and Fridays, you can work at the bar and serve tables. We open at nine p.m. and close at two a.m. You can keep the tips. I'll start you at ten dollars an hour."

"Look, I didn't come here to be a barmaid. I can do that anywhere. I came here to be a dancer."

He looked at Grace with contempt. "Look, you won't get tips like this anywhere else and all my dancers have to audition first so which is it going to be?"

"Are you serious?" Grace asked as she switched hips again and stood her ground.

"Yes I am. And you won't get hired anywhere else to be a barmaid because you must be twenty-one to serve alcohol."

"But, I just told you I'm twenty-nine."

"Okay." He smiled trying to catch her in a lying game. But, she smiled back which threw him off his game.

"Look, I just asked you to dance and you wouldn't, so what do you want from me?" He turned his back as if he was ignoring her. "Now, when you're ready to audition, come back to my office and I'll see what I can do."

She turned to leave. "Do I need a uniform to work the bar?"

"Nope. Just shorts or a short skirt—your choice. White shirt with a low cut front to show more cleavage, if you know what I mean. Shoes need to be heels, pumps, and open toe, but no flats."

"Okay, when do I start?"

"Tomorrow."

"Do I need to fill out any paperwork?"

He smiled. "Are you trying to get me locked up?"

"Look, I told you I am twenty-nine. If you don't believe me, that's your problem."

He just smiled and licked his lips as if he'd just eaten some whipped cream. "Oh, and you'll need a name tag. Will it be okay to put your real name on it or would you rather we make something up?"

He's being sarcastic now. "You can use my real name— Grace. And that is my name whether you believe me or not." She smiled and turned to leave. Maxi saw her leaving and pulled herself together. They both walked out closing the red door behind them and heading for the bar area which by now had filled up with patrons.

Chapter Four

——— *&* ———

The next day Maxi and Grace slept in through breakfast. By noon they were both ravished. Grace had slept in the guest bedroom, the size of her sons' room. Maxi had her master bedroom with the huge Jacuzzi bathroom and walk-in closets. It wasn't like Grace could afford a place of her own. When she'd fled her home in the past and didn't have a clue as to where she would end up, Maxi always came through and it always worked out.

Grace couldn't count the times she'd run away from her life as a mother and wife to a wonderful God-fearing husband. That didn't deter Grace from wanting to live in both worlds. Not that she didn't enjoy her married life. She loved Hilton. She adored her children. However, she just didn't have the same type of convictions, regrets, and morals as her husband did. Not yet anyway.

"Why do you think he wants me to start off as a waiter?" Grace couldn't believe Maxi hadn't spoke up to Levi on her behalf. "You should have told him how good I can dance," she said while putting on her makeup in the visor mirror in the car. "This is just not fair." They rode toward the shopping center. Their first stop was to Unique Thrift Store to pick out a few outfits for Grace's new position. Maxi agreed with Levi. Grace did look younger than her age. That's why she was going to need some wardrobe and makeup help to step up her game with Levi.

"I know, I know, and I agree. But Levi runs the club very differently than Ant did. Eventually he will let you dance. Like he said, you will definitely need to audition before he allows you up on his stage. And in case you don't know by now, Ace's is the biggest money making lounge and stage this side of Cleveland. Plus, working the bar will give you a chance to get back into the swing of things, see how he runs the club, and who's who."

Grace couldn't believe it was going to take all that to get back into her dance routine at Ace's. Maxi pulled up in front of the store. "Oh, and while it's on my mind, I'll tell you who you'll need to stay clear of. Now, there's a bunch of crazy bikers that come around, usually only on Friday nights. On several occasions the police had to be called because they're always packing heat with other bikers crossing the line."

"Oh really?" Grace said. "And what harm can they do besides get drunk and throw money up on that stage? And besides, I noticed there's a metal detector at the door and the bouncer looks intimidating, so how can anything get past him?"

"Yeah! Well, you will see for yourself," Maxi said. "Levi had that metal detector installed right after he took over the club. And the security guy at the door, he looks intimidating, but, believe me, he's as soft and gentle as a teddy bear. That's what I call him."

"Oh, really now? Grace said. "Sounds like you know from experience." They both broke out laughing.

"Yes, I do know first hand. He's a softy although he's good at keeping the riff-raff out. But sometimes things can get a little crazy when both biker gangs decide to show up on the same night. That's when things can get a little tricky for him."

"What biker gangs are out there? They never frequented Ace's in all the times I worked here before. So when did that start?"

"About a month after you left and Ant sold the club. Now that Levi owns it, there's a whole different crowd of people showing up. You'll see what I mean on Friday night."

———————

Later that night, they arrived back at the club right before nine o'clock. Levi was nowhere to be found, but there were others inside getting things set up for the Wednesday night crowd. Grace didn't have a clue about what it took to be a waitress. She was glad when one of the girls from the bar walked up and introduced herself.

"Hi. My name is Candi. Levi asked me to look out for the new girl. I take it that's you, right?"

"Yes, I'm Grace."

"Well, come on back, let me show you a few things. Put your purse and keys in this safe. Only open it before the club opens and after we close, and only the barmaids use this one. If you miss the cutoff you can use one of the lockers in the back. Here, wear this for your tips."

She tossed Grace a garter apron. She quickly slipped it on around her waist as three men approached them.

"Hey, guys, this is the new girl?"

"Grace, meet Tony, Winston, and Harley. Anybody mess with you, or their hands linger too long when they're giving you a tip, or being down right disrespectful, let these guys know immediately. They will handle it."

Grace smiled and shook their hands. Winston held on to her hand a little longer. "I'm sorry, but I got to ask. Didn't you work here before, as a dancer?" he said.

Grace nodded her head. "Yes. That was me."

"So, why are you back working as a barmaid? I remember how much money this place made when you were working for Anthony. Brought in tons of money on the nights you danced. So what gives?"

Grace smiled. "I don't know. I guess Levi is feeling me out to see if he can trust me or something. I told him I wanted to dance, but he insists I start off as a barmaid."

"Well, it's not that bad. He'll get you back up there soon enough. I'll talk to him. Meantime, if you ever need anything, you just let me know. They call me Daddy."

Grace smiled at his nickname. So he wanted to be called 'Daddy.' Okay, she could do that. By the end of the night Grace had spilled a million drinks and messed up just as many orders. But, she had made $250 in tips. Candi had told her once she got the hang of it, she would make more money. She found out the clientele for this club was pretty high class. As expected, she felt hands all over her pretty much all night. Men, wanting to feel on her behind. Maybe they didn't think it was real. Maybe they thought it was padding. After all, she did have more back there than most girls. That was her little secret to her dance routine, and with those strength training classes, she could work that pole like a tight rope.

Chapter Five

_____ *et* _____

After four weeks working at Ace's Club, Grace started getting the hang of things. She was bringing in somewhere between three and five hundred in tips alone, which was not bad. But, why did she need the money anyway? She didn't have a clue why she felt the need to make her own money. After all, Hilton took care of all the expenses and took very good care of her and the children. So why did she need to go back to this lifestyle, and for what? Late at nights she tossed and turned, sometimes not getting to sleep until early morning. She knew Hilton was probably on his knees praying she would come home. Hilton could show up any day and find her in some club. But after seeing her children, she often wondered to herself why she could ever go back out there. Her husband needed her; her children needed her. What was she running to or from?

Although it was lonely out there with no companionship except for Maxi, she knew better than to get involved with anyone. It would not only be dangerous for her, but for them as well. When Hilton decided it was time to make his move and come get her, it was always an ugly scene that she didn't want to put anyone through. Plus, she knew Hilton was within his rights to take his wife home, no matter how much money he had to pay.

It was after closing time when Grace was leaving the club. Maxi was taking too long, so she decided to wait in the car. She headed for the lockers to retrieve her purse and headed to the parking lot. As soon as she stepped outside she heard someone call her name. She turned her head toward the familiar voice only to see it was the security guy, Winston. She hadn't seen him all night. He was quite handsome and in the light of the parking lot she could see he was muscular, and with his shadow beard not quite growing in yet, he was definitely a good looking man; not to mention his smell lured her senses into every imagination possible.

Grace turned all the way around to face him. He approached her quickly and grabbed her arm. "Don't you ever walk out here alone like this any more! Do you hear me?" His touch seemed to burn her arm. She didn't know if it was just the sensation of him touching her or if it was something else, but it sent shock-waves through her. She looked up at him and pulled her arm slightly away. He repeated again, "It's too dangerous out here and I really don't want anything to happen, especially to you."

Was she expecting her husband Hilton to chase her down and rescue her every time she got herself into a situation? No. Hilton only came when, as he put it, his God prompted him to go out there into the world and find his wife and bring her back home. She was on her own this time.

"Okay. I won't," she said to Winston as she reluctantly turned to walk away, but she was drawn in by his scent. It was hypnotic like an aphrodisiac. She walked toward Maxi's car, and then turned to see if he was watching her walk away. He was. "Have a nice evening," she said. After getting inside the car, a glance in her rear-view mirror confirmed he was still standing there watching her. She couldn't see his face, but she was sure he was smiling. *"I wish I knew what he was thinking,"* she thought to herself.

Later that night she couldn't shake the image of his face from her mind. What was it about him that attracted her? Hilton was way better looking and had a body. But, he had confessed when she would leave on these trips, he didn't have time to go to the gym; what with the kids, the house, the chores, twice a week at church, and working a full time job, when would he have time?

If Maxi had met Hilton, she would've considered him a "bad boy," which he was far from. But Winston certainly was. He wore a leather biker vest with a short sleeve t-shirt under it and tight jeans with leather riding boots. He had tattoos covering his arms and a gold chain hung around his neck with a huge gold cross hanging from it. Hilton would never be caught dead in such apparel. To him that would have been considered "gaudy."

She decided she was probably always attracted to the bad boy type. That had to be the reason Winston's face burned into her mind all that night; not to mention her arm was still red hot from where he'd grabbed her in the parking lot and his smell seared into her nostrils forever.

———————————

After two months working as a waitress, having drinks spilled all over her and men grabbing on her as she walked by, it was getting old. From Grace's observation, the security guards were useless. They never came to her rescue when somebody got out of line. She had to fend off the wolves herself. Grace tried her best to avoid Winston. It wasn't that hard. When she was working, he was either in Levi's office or working security upstairs in the VIP Lounge. The VIP Lounge was on the second floor of the club, and you could only get in by special invitation. She remembered being up there plenty of times in her past dancing days; but a barmaid position only allowed her to work downstairs on the main floor.

Back when Anthony owned the club, if a huge crowd swelled up in the club, he would pull on her arm in between her dance routines and ask her to go up to the VIP and entertain his guest. She now wondered if Levi made his girls go upstairs on occasion. After all, there was a smaller dance stage up there to be used, which meant more hands groping; but you always left with more tips than you could count. Was it worth it? It all depended on who you were.

The dancer they called Sugarbaby was a single mom trying to get through college and taking care of her two little girls. She hated all the touching and groping. As for Babydoll, another dancer with big round eyes that made her look like a big baby doll, she was taking care of her elderly mother and just needed enough money to pay her car note; plus, she had recently divorced and lost her children and home to the custody of her husband. His lawyer had a private investigator secretly taking pictures of her dancing at the club, and leaving the kids home alone. She'd swear they were asleep before she left the apartment, and her neighbor across the hall was supposed to look in on them. But, she lost the case and her children.

And then there was Maxi, which was her stage name. Maxi was a single white female with no children. Enrolled in a community college with future plans to become a nurse, she said the money paid for her rent plus tuition. She was able to take at least one lavish vacation every year with her girlfriends and she ate out almost every night. Maxi boasted she didn't need a man to survive. She loved her singleness and wouldn't have it any other way. Her motto was, "I'm every woman."

But, as for Grace, she had no idea why she was even out there. She didn't need the money. For some reason the pull of the world drew her back into dancing. She loved to dance. To Grace it was a form of art. But, so far she had no luck convincing Levi to allow her to dance as back up on that stage. Eventually, she knew the only way she would dance was to audition in the privacy of his office. She wasn't looking forward to that.

One Friday night when she arrived at the club, Winston stopped her as soon as she walked in the door. "Good evening, Grace." He smiled and hugged her up to him. She pulled back slightly, but not before she got a waft of his cologne. It almost made her dizzy—in a good way. Was she falling for this man? "The boss wants to see you in his office now."

"What? Why? I mean, what did I do?"

"I don't know. I'm just passing on his message. As soon as you arrive he said to have you come back to see him. That's all I know."

A hundred things were running through her mind. Was he going to fire her? Did some money come up missing? Was he cutting her hours? She didn't know what to think, which made her nervous. She just wished Hilton was praying for her right now. She knew it was wrong to think that God would intervene in her situation. But, just in case she was in trouble, she wanted some sort of protection. Hilton had tried to teach her about the things of God, and how He was a protector in the times of trouble; a person to hide behind if you needed to be hidden.

Knock, knock.

"Come on in." It was Levi's voice. There were two other girl dancers in the room with him. One was sitting on his lap, and the other one was standing behind him with her arms draped around his neck whispering something into his ears.

"Hello, Grace. How's it going so far?"

"Great," she said. "Is everything alright?"

"Yes. I have no complaints." He took a long pull from his beer bottle. "Tonight I want you to go upstairs and serve from the bar in the VIP Lounge." She looked at him sideways but didn't say a word.

"Can you do that for me?" He wasn't paying any attention to the girls who were falling all over him. It was disgusting. She could never see herself drooling over Levi. Never.

"Yes, I can do that. Do you want me to work upstairs for the entire night?"

"Yes. And thank you. I'll come up later to see how things are going."

"Okay. See ya' later." She turned and left his office.

Whew! A few minutes later she ran into Maxi in the ladies' room and told her about her new assignment. "Girl, that is great. That means he likes you, Grace. He never allows the other girls from the floor to work upstairs in VIP. You must have made a good impression on him so far. Plus, your tips will be over the top up there."

They both smiled at the thought of her apron pockets overflowing with tip money. "I guess that's a good thing, right?"

"You best believe it's a good thing. Girl, Chaunte, Princess, and Candi will be furious. They've worked here for over a year now and have never been asked to work the VIP section. Yes, he definitely sees something special in you."

Grace didn't see anything special in being a barmaid. She loved the atmosphere and the attention the men gave her, but she didn't like their hands on her, although that's what got her more tip money. What she really wanted to do was dance.

She had thought about doing this for a couple weeks now and decided to talk with Maxi about her little plan. After this act, she knew for sure Levi would let her dance. But, for now she would make him happy by working the VIP and line her apron pockets with his VIP money.

Chapter Six

—— *et* ——

The first thing she noticed in the VIP Lounge was how the women threw themselves at Winston, literally. It was ridiculous, but she definitely couldn't blame them. Every blue moon one would get lucky and he would go in the back with her where there were more private offices. Levi had done a huge upgrade in the VIP Lounge, different than when she was last up there a year ago. It was more elegant with a classy touch, a romantic atmosphere. The more romance, the more men to entice those dollar bills.

At one point when Winston went toward the back with another girl, Grace had the audacity to be jealous. Imagine that! Since the night of the parking lot incident, she still could not get his smell out of her nostrils and his face out of her mind. Every once in a while he would let her catch him staring at her, but he never said anything out of the way.

It was Friday night, one of the busiest nights on the main floor as well as the VIP Lounge. She hadn't seen Levi come upstairs yet to check on her. Things were going well, the money was flowing, music was playing, when all of a sudden two guys ascended the stairs and stopped to slowly take a look around. From the dark lights, she thought for sure it was Hilton. He had finally come to get her and drag her out of this place—again. She froze in her tracks like a deer caught in headlights. Finally, one of them walked toward the bar and she could tell it was not Hilton, but by the time she realized it, her heart was about to pop out of her chest.

Winston spotted Grace from across the room. He slowly made his way over to the bar and pulled up a stool. He could see she was busy. The club was packed, and Levi had allowed more and more of his friends to come upstairs to the VIP Lounge. Sugarbaby was dancing on the small stage working the pole. It wasn't as big of a venue as the downstairs floor. But still, you could get quite a few people packed in up there.

Winston noticed Grace had abruptly stopped in her tracks after noticing the two men coming from downstairs. *Did she know them?* he wondered. From the look on her face, it looked like she'd seen a ghost. A few minutes later, they moved further into the room and disappeared toward the stage where Sugarbaby was dancing with a wad of money in their hands.

He took this opportunity to move up behind Grace. He could tell something was on her mind. *"Boo!"* She jumped straight up and dropped her tray filled with empty beer bottles. "Oh, I am so sorry. I didn't mean to scare you like

52

that." They both bent down at the same time and started picking up the bottles. Thank God nothing was broken, or Levi would have her back downstairs on the main floor before the night was over. "My bad! I am so sorry," Winston said as he touched her arm while they were still bent down.

"It's okay. Really. I need to take a break anyway," she said as they gathered up the bottles from the floor. Grace tried her best to sort out her feelings. She made her way downstairs and to the back where the private employee bathroom was located. What was the deal with this guy, Winston, anyway? Was he really into her? She knew for a fact that the majority of the men in the club would love for her to be around them. She would just have to keep a watch out for him sneaking up on her again.

Somebody else had come into the 'Employee Only' ladies room. Grace flushed and unlocked the stall door only to find Sugarbaby standing at the sink with tears running down her heavily made up face. "What's wrong, sweetheart? What happened to you?" Grace pulled a few paper towels from the container and helped her dry her hands and face. By the time her tears stopped flowing her makeup was ruined.

"I just can't do this anymore. I know it's wrong, but it pays my bills. I just can't take these men pulling and groping all over me. It's disgusting." She started crying all over again.

Grace grabbed and pulled her into a tight hug. "Don't worry. When Levi hears about them touching you, he'll get it all straightened out." Grace tried to soothe her. "I thought he was supposed to have security guards in place to make sure they don't touch you. Were any of them around?"

"I don't know," she said in tears again. "I didn't see any of them. I was just trying to get through my routine. But, it's always the same when Levi asks me to dance the VIP. I would rather dance down on the main floor." Sugarbaby dabbed at her face again, but with her makeup smeared, it was obvious she wasn't going back out on the floor—not tonight, not without makeup, not with her hair tossed back and out of place, not with her completely and emotionally drained.

"Do you need me to go in with you to see Levi to let him know what's going on?" For some reason Grace felt empathy for this young girl. She knew all too well how these men could be when they got drunk, but Anthony used that to his advantage. The drunker they got, the more money they threw up on the stage and he always got his cut of whatever the girls picked up from the floor at the end of her routine. But she wasn't sure how Levi did things. Obviously, the security in VIP was slacking. Winston had been upstairs when she came down. Why didn't he see what was going on? He was working security, wasn't he? No. He was having his own needs met in the back room. This just didn't make any sense.

"No. I'm not going to talk to Levi tonight. I'm going home. I'll talk to him tomorrow night. If anybody asks, tell them I got sick and had to leave." Sugarbaby looked deflated. When she was upstairs working that pole, she was so full of vigor and energy. Grace loved her routine. It reminded her of when she was dancing. Sugarbaby was limber and could flex her body into weird positions. The crowd loved when she did so. But, Grace knew she could dance even better than that. If only Levi gave her a chance.

Grace returned to the VIP Lounge to find Maxi dancing in place of Sugarbaby. She resumed her role as barmaid. It was jam-packed upstairs, compliments of Levi. She could tell some were first time VIP guests, but most knew the drill.

The room was full of cigarette smoke. She didn't know why Levi had allowed his guests to smoke up there. Ant would have never allowed that. It was against the law. He had a rule that all smokers had to light up outside. There were smoke detectors all over the place, but her guess was no one had changed the batteries in those detectors over time, and that's why they never went off.

Grace spotted Winston as soon as she reached the top step in VIP. He was sitting on one of the leather couches with the same two girls hanging on his arms. Why hadn't he been standing over by the dance stage, watching those bullies reaching and groping on Sugarbaby. It looked like they were doing the same thing to Maxi now, but from where she stood, Maxi seemed to be handling herself pretty well. She knew how to get them off of her, but not push them away. After all, it was all about the money and the more she showed and revealed under that skirt, the more money went flying through the air on stage.

As she was putting in another round of drink orders, someone tapped her on the shoulder. She instantly turned around to address Winston. "What do you want now?" But, it wasn't Winston. It was Levi.

"Everything going okay?" He smiled wide, revealing a row of pearly whites. She never realized how white his teeth were until seeing them in the lights upstairs in the VIP. Her eyes went straight to his lips and then back up to his eyes. She hoped he wasn't getting the wrong signal from her stare.

"I'm sorry. I thought you were someone else. Yes, everything is going great." She swallowed to wet her throat. "By the way, Sugarbaby came down ill with something. She was sick in the bathroom and had to leave."

"Yeah, Harley told me he had to escort her out to her car. He said she looked awful. She did the right thing by leaving. I'm glad Maxi didn't mind filling in for her up here."

"Levi, can I ask you a question?" She shifted her weight to her other leg, still balancing her drink tray in both hands, and realizing her feet were killing her from the stiletto heels she had been running around in all night.

"If it's about letting you dance, this is not the time or the place," he shot back.

"No, it's not about that. I was going to ask you about the security up here."

"Security? You just worry about serving drinks and let me worry about my security, okay?" He turned to walk away, but she wasn't letting him get away that fast.

"So, what is Winston's role while he's up here?"

"Winston? Why are you so concerned about what my employees do? They work for me, not you. I pay their salaries, not you. They do what I tell them to do, and I make the schedules, I hire, I fire, and so forth. Now, if you got any more questions about how I run my business, I suggest you come see me in my office."

Grace couldn't believe he had gotten loud with her on the VIP floor. She knew from the faces in the crowd they had overheard Levi reprimanding her. She was embarrassed and furious. She couldn't wait until her shift was over to get out of there.

"Oh, and by the way, I need you to close tonight," Levi said before walking away.

Grace frowned but quickly found her voice. "But, but I don't close."

"Well, you do now. Get with Candi. She'll stay with you and show you how." And with that he disappeared back into the crowd.

She was hotter than a fire cracker, but she kept her cool for the rest of the night. She took drink orders, loaded her drink tray, cleared tables, rung up tabs, made change, pocketed her tips, and repeated the same routine all night. It was close to two o'clock when Candi grabbed her arm and told her they needed to start counting and cashing out the drawers. But, before they made it back down to the main floor, Tony pushed his way through the crowd looking for Levi, and as soon as he saw him they knew it was not good.

"Sorry boss, but we got a situation downstairs."

Chapter Seven

——————— *et* ———————

The music from downstairs, which also ran the speakers to the upstairs lounge, had stopped. Someone had either turned off the power, or there was a city power failure. Loud voices were coming from downstairs and the guests were leaving in a hurry. Grace wanted to see what all the commotion was about.

Maxi scanned the crowd until she spotted Grace with Candi. "Come on, girls, follow me. We got to get in one of the back rooms and lock down. Something is jumping off downstairs, and when that happens, security usually clears the place out."

"But what could possibly be going on down there that we can't leave out the same door as everybody else?" Grace was still holding her drink tray filled with empty glasses, bottles, and money.

"Not an option. Now put that tray down and come on."

"Now?"

"Yes, now!" Maxi shouted at the top of her lungs. Grace and Candi knew she meant business.

While most of the crowd was tripping over each other trying to make it down the stairs, Maxi, Candi, and Grace pushed their way toward the back of the VIP Lounge and ran down the hall to the last room where they locked and bolted the door. Maxi pushed a dresser across the door for added security and together they crouched down on the floor next to a bed and waited. None of the girls wanted to sit on the bed. No telling who had just finished doing their business in there.

_____

After what seemed like a life time of waiting, someone finally came upstairs and knocked on the door. Maxi motioned for them not to say anything. Again, a knock at the door. Finally someone spoke. "Maxi, it's me. Let me in. You can come out now." The person waited a few minutes then knocked again, only this time a little harder. "Grace, are you in there? Open the door. It's me, Daddy. Everything is okay. Now, open the door please."

As soon as she heard him say it was "Daddy," she knew it was definitely Winston. Grace bolted for the door. Pushing the dresser to the side, she unlocked it and there stood Winston. She didn't hesitate to fly into his arms.

"Oh, my God, that was so scary. What happened?" She was shaking like a leaf and even though his big arms were wrapped securely around her, she couldn't control the shaking. She pressed her body up against his.

"Are you cold?"

"No, why?"

"Because you're shivering."

Maxi and Candi pushed past him. "Where is Levi?"

"He's not here right now. Had to make an emergency run. He left me in charge, and it looks like everybody else is gone but you three and myself. Now, let's get this place in order and locked up for the night. Is that okay, girls?"

They didn't have much choice if they wanted to keep their jobs. Nobody questioned him as to what had transpired and why the place had cleared out so suddenly. Winston made sure all the money was locked in the safe and the chairs turned upside down on the tables. He bagged all the garbage and made ten trips out to the dumpster before walking them out to their cars. Candi took off before they had a chance to wave goodbye. By the time Maxi and Grace crawled into bed it was after four in the morning.

———————

The next day was Saturday and neither one of them had to work. They slept in until the bed rejected them. Grace was the first to get up. She made a pot of coffee, found some eggs, milk and bread—enough to make two stacks of French toast for both of them. Grace's three children loved French toast. She pushed back the lump in her throat as the image of Hilton's face flashed before her eyes.

Thankfully, Maxi was finally stirring. She opened her eyes.

"Good morning, sleepy head. Made us some breakfast," Grace said.

"Oh, my. What time is it?"

"It's lunch time, but who's keeping track," Grace said. "Let's get dressed and get out in the sun. I refuse to stay locked up in this apartment all day. It's eighty degrees out already."

"Whoa! You're moving too fast for me," Maxi said. She followed her nostrils into the kitchen and pulled out a plate, put three slices of French toast on it, found some syrup in the cabinet and poured it on heavy. After her second cup of coffee, she was finally ready for a shower and some sunshine.

"Hey, let's call Candi to see if she wants to hang out with us," Maxi said. "Besides, that was some messed up drama going on at the club last night. I hope Levi calls a meeting like he always does when stuff like this jumps off, just to fill us in. But, until then, let's forget about it and get out and have some fun."

A few hours later they were on their way to Candice's place. Candi lived in a gated community in Beachwood, an upper class neighborhood where there was still old money to be spent. Candi drove a beautiful new pearly white

Mercedes. She and Jeffrey were transplants from Las Vegas. Born and raised in Las Vegas, Candice had lived there her whole childhood. Her father was a longtime resident, having spent thirty years in building and overseeing the maintenance of casino pools. She remembered his famous tip to vacationers: *Stay away from pools known for hosting big late-night parties. Chlorine can only do so much.*

She had met her now husband, Jeffrey, who climbed the ranks and was a huge developer in Vegas. Together they purchased several buildings and Jeffrey frequently traveled back and forth closing deals and making new ones. The business was quite profitable which afforded Candi to spend money like there was no tomorrow. She spared no expense when it came to her wardrobe and living comfortable— designer everything. Her exquisite condo was furnished with top of the line designer furniture, some of which was flown in from Italy.

But it had been years since Candi lived in Vegas. She and Jeffrey had moved to Ohio to start fresh after an almost ugly divorce. Somehow they managed to work things out. The move had proven to be good for their marriage, however, the business kept Jeff going back and forth to Vegas every week.

On the way over to Candi's, Maxi mentioned to Grace how Candi lived a very lonely life while Jeffrey traveled, which explained why Candi had allowed her youngest sister, Brandi, to move in with her. But, it still puzzled Maxi why Candi felt the need to work in a low life club like Ace's. She had all the money she needed and then some. She could work at any club in Vegas, a few of which she owned with her husband.

Once they got through the security gate, Candi buzzed them in. They walked past a full workout center filled with exercise machines and sweaty tenants in the midst of their afternoon workout routines. They took the elevator to the twelfth floor where Candi was waiting in her doorway at the end of the hall. They hugged each other and Maxi went straight to the bar and pulled out the blender. She made a pitcher of Cosmopolitans and poured each of them a glass. They headed out to the patio overlooking the pool below. From the twelfth floor you could see for miles and miles across town and around the development.

"So," Candi said, "what do you think of all the commotion at the club last night?"

"Girl, we did not come all the way over here to talk about Ace's Lounge. Let's just hang out and then go shopping or something." Maxi did not want to talk about Levi again until she had to report back to work.

"Well, I was just thinking, it was very strange that Levi was not there when the smoke cleared. He just up and left Winston in charge. That just doesn't make any sense to me. But, oh well. So you all want to talk about something else, let's talk about Jeffrey and how he has not been home in weeks. Claims he's still in Vegas taking care of business."

"Now, Candi, will you stop this. You living like you're rich, and you sit here and complain. Do you know I can just barely pay my rent with what Levi pays me! My tuition is going up at school, and my car needs a lot of work." Maxi looked around and then back at Candi. "You're living up here like a goddess with every name brand piece of furniture, clothing line, and a luxury car and you are complaining?"

She let that sink in for a minute. "And why in the world do you even waste your time working at Ace's Lounge. That hole in the wall. You have everything you need right here. So what gives with you? I mean, is Jeffrey taking care of business or what?"

"I'm sorry, girls. I guess I can be ungrateful at times."

"At times? Now that's an understatement." They all burst out laughing and took another drink from their glasses.

Candi moved her chair closer to the edge to look out over the pool area. "So, Grace, you say you want to dance; you should consider moving to Vegas. Girl, you'll have no problem finding a gig in the 'City of Lights.' She looked at Grace and all three of them took long drinks from their Cosmos. Where was all this coming from? Candi was trying to change the subject. But could she really tell that Grace sometimes wished she could run away to dance in Vegas? Although Candi was full of righteous rage because of her past hurt and pain caused by Jeffrey, how could she see inside the heart of a person like Grace?

"Yes. Vegas is a magical mystery town where anything could happen, and it usually does," Candi stated. They all laughed but Grace's face lit up. She wanted to hear more about this place called the City of Lights.

"Go on… tell me more."

"Well, it's hard to explain," Candi said. "For instance, take their call girls; they are very obliging creatures, ready for action at all times. The money to be made in Vegas is phenomenal. I'm talking a six figure income, girl."

"And how do you know so much about this?" Maxi asked. Not that she was interested but it sounded intriguing.

"Because Jeffrey told me what the girls at our clubs make. Plus, we've met two of the girls that work at Caesar Palace, one name Yvette, a petite, Asian woman, and another girl name Fantasy, a big breasted black beauty that resembles Naomi Campbell. They both own their own yachts and have access to private planes while traveling back and forth to Paris."

———————

Candi took another drink from her Cosmopolitan as she thought about the big beautiful home she and Jeffrey still owned together—a beautiful $3 million dollar home in Vegas.

Jeffrey had purchased the home from a well-known rock star, and within a month, they'd worked out the details and exchanged funds. The home was equipped with state-of-the-art features such as accent lighting, skylights, an elevator, and large pocket doors for merging indoor-outdoor living spaces. Five bedrooms and six baths, including a master suite with its own fireplace, along with a $300,000 movie theater with 3D projector, an insane surround sound system along with a 65-inch flat screen television that rose from beneath a slate deck with the click of a remote.

As if that weren't enough, the home included a decked-out entertainment room with custom lighting and a fully equipped home gym. Furthering the resort-like feel of the property, Jeffrey loved the telescoping walls of glass with a view of the outdoor spaces that included a backyard oasis with a disappearing-edge pool and a magnificent view of the Las Vegas Strip.

Before Jeffrey splurged on the mansion, Candi had worked four days a week as a dancer at the Flamingo and had made a ton of money. With her long jet-black hair and smooth olive skin she'd been quite the center of attraction. Men could not get enough of her. But after taking a position over at Caesar Palace, she accidentally met her husband, Jeffrey Somers, on an elevator and he didn't waste any time making his move. He'd swept her out of Vegas so fast and claimed her for himself.

She remembered Jeffrey had a best friend named Griffith, who stood trial on charges that he killed a famous Vegas dancer, Fantasy. She was a dancer for the Cirque du Soleil show at The Mirage. Griffith had pleaded not guilty to first-degree murder of Fantasy. His attorney said the evidence only showed that Griffith had a history of violence against women. He defended him and was able to negotiate a plea deal for Griffith not to face the death penalty, but instead, he got life in prison. Jeffrey had said Fantasy was into erotica dominance submission role playing and anything could have happened to her—by accident, of course.

Because Jeffrey had a passion for beautiful women like Fantasy, Candi would not share her man with any of them and had threatened to leave him and file for a divorce. Consequently, he got it together and piled up the gifts and expensive jewelry to keep her happy. She couldn't explain why, but she had allowed herself to be dazzled, even though she had her own secret off shore bank account. Yet, it was mysterious and exciting to be married to Jeffrey Somers— almost like a fairy tale come true. Without a thought, she'd accepted his proposal to marry and relocate to Ohio, leaving behind her Vegas life for good. She hadn't thought much about it until now.

"A private yacht and Paris," Grace repeated, pulling Candi back from the past. "Must be nice to live a life of such luxury and freedom. And, what about you, Candi?"

Suddenly the sliding glass doors opened and out stepped another beauty queen onto the patio. She was much younger than Candi, but the spitting image of her. About nineteen at the most, but drop-dead gorgeous with long jet-black hair, and white dazzling shades sitting on top of her head. Her skin was beautiful and tanned with huge dangling hoop earrings and her neck draped with a cascade of chains. She wore bangles that tinkled with every move she made. Her loose sleeveless top hung down over her black leggings, with a wide black belt that fastened with a huge white bow in front. Her purse and matching heels were no doubt designer name brand. Taking in the full picture made her look much older than she really was. She was absolutely stunning. Not to mention she drove around town in a red drop top sports car.

"What's up, Aunt Maxi?" Brandi said. "Hey, Candi, and…" She hesitated and stared at Grace. "I'm sorry; I don't remember your name. Have we met?"

"No, I don't believe so. I'm Grace. Nice to meet you."

"Nice to meet you as well. I'm Brandi, Candi's little sister. Are you from around here?"

Grace was surprised. She thought this young girl might have been Candi's daughter, not her sister. Grace wasn't comfortable answering personal questions. She would never tell how she really ended up back in Cleveland. "No, I'm not actually from around here, and yes, I'm staying with Maxi right now. We work together down at Ace's."

"Oh. Well, looks like that's the place to be on Friday nights."

Candi immediately sat up in her chair. "And, young lady, I better not catch you up in there. I've told you before, that is no place for you or your friends." Candi downed the rest of her drink as she checked her sister again. "Besides, you are always trying to act like you're so grown."

"I know. I know. I'm not coming down there anytime soon. Why would I, especially while you're working there?

Besides, if I wanted to get in, I could," Brandi said as she sat her Prada purse down and kicked off her red bottom heels.

"Well, like I said, you're not old enough to get in there, number one, and, I better never hear about you down there even if you are of age." Candi held up her empty glass. "Now, go inside and make us another pitcher of Cosmopolitans. And, did you pick up my dry cleaning like I asked you to?"

Candi had to act as a mother to her little sister ever since Brandi had turned eighteen and thought she was grown enough to leave their mother's home in Chicago and move to Cleveland. But after trying to live out on her own for a few months, Jeffrey ended up having to go get her and bring all of her things to their place in Beachwood. Of course, Candi didn't want any of Brandi's old things brought to her condo. So, she donated it all to Salvation Army and gave Candi the lavish guest bedroom. That was three years ago. Since then, their mother had passed away and it was just the two of them. Jeffrey agreed to give Brandi anything she wanted if she could keep his wife company while he was away. It was one of their many unspoken rules but all three of them knew it was a fact. Candi was content, Brandi was happy, and Jeffrey did his thing. And so, life went on.

Little did Candi know, but her little sister had talked Jeffrey into throwing her twenty-first birthday party at the Plaza Hotel in Vegas. It was already being planned and invitations ordered. Jeffrey had already scheduled for his private plane to pick her up with a bunch of her friends, and the ones who couldn't come with them were meeting them in Vegas at the hotel. She had the entire twenty-first floor blocked off for her family and friends with a pool party that Friday night. Of course, Candi was going to have a fit when she found out. But it would already be too late by then.

Chapter Eight

—— *&* ——

Brandi was only twenty years old but could somehow or another wrangle her way into any night club in Cleveland she wanted to. Fake ID? No problem. Lavish tips to the doormen? No problem. Cultivating a friendship with one of the promoters? No problem. When it came to getting in anywhere, she could do it. Some knew she was Candi's little sister, the wife of the rich and famous Jeffrey Somers from Vegas.

Brandi's two best friends, Sammie, short for Samantha, and Jessie, the gay son of a well known jazz singer who performed every weekend at the Jazz Club in downtown Cleveland, made plans every weekend to hook up and hang out. Then there was Zach, her on again, off again boyfriend who was not so pleased with Brandi hanging out with her girlfriends every weekend. The night life was not for him. He was not into drinking or doing drugs, and he hated the night scene. But Brandi loved every minute of it. Not that she drank or did drugs, but she did like hanging around people who did. She got a kick watching people make fools out of themselves.

She brought the pitcher of freshly made Cosmopolitan drinks out onto the balcony and pulled up a chair to the table where Maxi, Grace, and Candi were still chatting, as if they were going to allow her into their conversation.

"So, where are we going tonight?" she asked, knowing that would piss her sister off.

"Umm… excuse me, little girl," Candi replied. "You're not going anywhere with us. I keep telling you, you're too young. Plus, who said we were going anywhere?" It was getting harder to control her baby sister. The closer she got to turning twenty-one, the more she had to check her actions.

Brandi pulled out her Chanel compact to reapply her lipstick. "I was just kidding, but, seriously, where are *you* divas hanging out tonight?" Who was she kidding or did she really think they would tell her anything, even if they were planning to go out.

Candi would never give Brandi her itinerary even though Jeff insisted it was a good idea, just in case something happened. But, she refused to be caught dead in a club where her little sister was hanging out. Not that it hadn't occurred to her that Brandi was turning twenty-one in three months and could get into any club. But, thank God she had a little while before she had to worry about that—so she thought.

Brandi had already gotten past Winston, Tony, and Harley at Ace's Lounge. They knew she was Candi's little sister, but money talked every time. Thankfully for Brandi, she had somehow managed to dodge her sister working the VIP floor on the nights she had gotten in.

———————

Grace was lost in her thoughts. Staring out over the balcony at a family down by the pool area as their children played in the water with inner tubes and water balls, she couldn't help but wonder what her children were doing and who was playing with them. What had Hilton told them when they asked why mommy was gone? She felt a tinge of guilt, but not enough to get up and go back to that life. No, it wasn't easy leaving her children, and she did love Hilton. But, there was always that inner struggle pulling her back into the world. It was a constant battle in her mind, and almost all the time she lost.

And then there was Winston. Had he felt anything more about her last night as he held her in his arms? After all, she was shivering but she was not cold. That whole incident with the club clearing out like it was some sort of raid, and with all the commotion on the main floor had left her shaken.

She could tell it was frightening to Maxi and Candi, both hovering together on the floor in a barricaded back room, but Candi was the first to finally relax as if this was routine. They eventually recovered from almost having a heart attack. But it still felt good when the door finally opened and she was safely wrapped up in Winston's arms.

"Penny for your thoughts!" Maxi said. Grace snapped out of her trance.

"Who me?" Grace turned her attention back to the ladies. "I was just thinking about last night. I know you guys don't want to talk about it, but stuff like that would have never happened when Anthony owned the Ace. I mean ..."

"Yes, you are right," Candi interjected. "But that was before those biker gangs started hanging out down there on Friday nights. I keep telling Levi he needs to beef up his security."

"Speaking of security, did you know one of the dancers, Sugarbaby, had to leave last night? I ran into her in the ladies room around midnight. She was upset and crying when I came out of the stall."

"Why? What happened?" Candi and Maxi sat up to get the whole story. Brandi had earlier excused herself from their conversation and had gone back inside. Grace took a long drink from her glass and continued.

"Well, from what I can gather, Levi had asked her to dance up in VIP, and I guess the men got too close and were groping and feeling all over her. It got to be too overwhelming at some point, so she left the stage and came downstairs to the ladies room. She was a mess."

"Wow," Maxi said. "Where is security when you need them? That is not acceptable. Does Levi know about this?"

"Yes, he does. I bumped into him back up in VIP and when I mentioned Sugarbaby was sick and had to leave, he said he already knew."

"Wow," Maxi said. "I was wondering why he pulled me from the main floor to go upstairs to dance. I really can't stand it up there to be honest with you. There is never any security, and yes, you make a lot of money in tips, but the men touching and groping can get out of hand," Maxi said. "I remember the one time I had to smack this guy for trying to pull on me and wouldn't let me go. There was no security around so I smacked him, hard. He backed away but if looks could kill…"

"Well, you ladies need to let Levi know when these sort of things happen," Candi said. "It's his club and he is supposed to provide adequate security for all the dancers. That's part of the deal," she said. "He wouldn't get away with that if he was in Vegas. No, siree. You can ask Jeffrey. Those clubs provide top notch round the clock protection."

"Well, I did see Winston upstairs, but he wasn't working security, at least it didn't appear to me," Grace said. "He had two ladies lapping all over him like a hungry dog." They all burst out laughing.

"Yeah, well he seemed to be sweet on you also last night, Grace," Candi said with a smirk on her face. Grace knew they would eventually bring up how she'd run into his arms as soon as the door opened. "I didn't know you guys were that friendly?"

"No. Not me. I don't know him at all like that; other than when Maxi introduced us and last night when he bumped into me on the floor spilling all my drinks, which was a big mess to clean up. But he did hang around and help me. Other than that…"

Grace was not admitting to having feelings for Winston, especially with Maxi knowing she was married with children. Not that it mattered. Nobody seemed to care that she was working at a bar and had walked away from her wonderful life to work at Ace's Lounge. Who in their right mind would do anything like that anyway?

"I'm just calling it like I see it," Candi said. "That's all I got to say." Grace was very glad when they changed the subject back to Jeffrey and his business ventures in Vegas, which ended up with Candi telling them about all the shopping at the high end stores at the Cosmopolitan Hotel.

Chapter Nine

— *et* —

It was finally Monday. Maxi and Grace had to be at work that night. Grace decided it was time to let Maxi in on her plan. She knew she would have to audition for Levi if she wanted to dance, but she had a different approach. They agreed that Wednesday was the best day to pull it off. Four months of working the floor carrying heavy drink trays was enough for Grace. She wanted to dance.

"Do you think you can do it?" Maxi asked. It had been a year since Grace had danced professionally, and every now and then Maxi and Candi would catch Grace staring at the dance stage like it was calling her name.

"Are you kidding me?" Grace said. "Dancing is my middle name. Plus, I've been secretly practicing my moves."

"So then, why don't you just audition for Levi in his office and get it over with?"

"Because that's too easy. I want him to approach me and ask me to dance, but he has to see what I can do and I plan to prove it Wednesday night. But, I'll need your help."

"My help? What do you want me to do?" Maxi asked, perplexed because two girls never did a routine together on stage at the same time. This was going to be interesting.

Maxi was shorter and thicker. She'd worked at Ace's long enough to know what excited the men and what didn't. She was one of the few that Levi kept around after Anthony had been long gone. Almost all of the staff had been replaced when Levi took over the club. Maxi also knew how to work the floor as a barmaid, which made her an asset to Levi. Plus, she was always available when someone called in sick or just didn't show up. Wednesday night finally arrived. There was always a bigger crowd than Monday nights, but nothing was like a Friday night at Ace's Lounge.

Grace fell into her regular routine serving tables. The usual Wednesday crowd was there. Same sleazy guys groping her as she walked past, or trying to squeeze her from behind to see if it was real. One guy even tried to slide his hand under her short mini skirt. Grace immediately checked him with a threat she'd have Levi ban him from ever coming back to the club. He kept his hands to himself after that.

Sugarbaby was looking beautiful as ever. Sugarbaby didn't mind dancing on the main floor. She just didn't want to go back upstairs to VIP, and had made that clear to Levi. Honeybun finally came onstage after Sugarbaby, and the crowd was really getting into her, which to Grace was quite boring.

Grace had made sure to take an extra set of clothes to work that night to change into for her performance. Tony was doing security that night, but everybody knew he did more flirting than checking the doors for weapons and drugs. He was checking out the ladies and exchanging digits instead.

Grace made friendly talk to the patrons and finally spotted Levi and Winston walking through the club headed for the back office. Winston caught her stare and winked. She didn't want to smile but it was involuntary. How could she not smile at this beautiful specimen?

The night was almost over and the crowd was starting to thin out. It was getting close to closing time. Time for Grace to pull off her little stunt. She pulled Maxi aside to let her know it was time. They had already cued in DJ Jimmy Jazz to hang around five minutes later so he could play the right song and run the stage lights. Candi said she was in on it also, but she had no idea exactly what was going down. She agreed to be the lookout person. "I'll tell you if anybody is coming," she said.

A few minutes later when Grace and Maxi walked up the back steps and onto the stage, Grace felt like she had finally made it home. This was where she belonged. She loved to dance. Maxi was right behind her with a folding chair. They both had changed into a more provocative outfit with tall black patent leather boots, black long sleeved lace gloves, and their makeup was heavy and gothic for this routine.

She knew all the other dancers, Sugarbaby, Honeybun, and Babydoll, were still in the back changing clothes to leave.

Levi and Winston were back in the big office. Tony and Harley were conversing at the door with a few patrons who were still lingering around. The music suddenly started and Grace slowly sashayed over to the pole at the far left side of the stage. She started to swing around the pole, and then did an upright split on the pole while holding her own weight upside down. Before she could get further into her routine, Tony and Harley had disappeared to the back office to inform Levi as to what was going down out front.

"You should seriously consider letting Grace dance!" Tony said.

Levi looked up and then at Winston and frowned. "And why would I do that?" he asked.

"Because she's good!"

"And how do you know this?"

"Go see for yourself; she's onstage now."

They both immediately got up from their chairs and walked out to the lounge area where the music was already playing the song, "How to Love," Grace's favorite song to dance to. Levi immediately noticed both Grace and Maxi on stage. Maxi was sitting in a chair with her arms tied up with a rope and blindfolded. They both were dressed in all black gothic attire. Sugarbaby came from the back along with the other dancers. They couldn't believe what they were seeing.

Grace immediately remembered her strength training classes and turned her body upside down into another split on the length of the pole, then into an upright stand. She was amazed her arms could still support the weight of her body.

She flipped herself around on the pole and back over moving very slow, then slid down to the floor like a fireman. As she neared the bottom she slid into a full split for a few seconds at the bottom allowing her behind to bounce up and down on the floor a few times before turning around and leaned her back against the pole then slinked back up slowly. Next she snaked her way back up grabbing the pole and wrapping one leg around it swinging before grabbing it with one hand and spinning around and around.

At this point she walked seductively up to Maxi and stood with one leg between Maxi's legs and raised one leg to push the chair back slightly. She grabbed the rope from around Maxi's wrist and untied it. Next she pretended to give Maxi two lashes as if she was being forced into submission for special effects.

She walked behind the chair where Maxi was still sitting and slowly danced around until she gently pulled the blind fold off Maxi's eyes and tilted the chair backwards as if she was going to let it fall. She then finally let it go. Maxi got up and at this point she exited the stage with the chair and her props.

The song began to fade as Grace walked back to the pole and did a full swing with her leg and arm that went into another full split upright on the pole and then slowly flipped upside down again, turning her body around until she slid to the bottom and like a snake crawled across the floor on her belly towards the edge of the stage, which was where all the men would be standing and cheering, throwing money towards her. When the music finally stopped, she slowly opened her eyes and her heart almost jumped out of her skin.

So much for Candi being the look out. Maxi was standing next to the DJ Jimmy Jazz, who was giving her two thumbs up. Suddenly, she heard clapping. It was Levi, Winston, Tony, Harley, and three of the other dancers all clapping for her performance. Winston had a silly grin on his face. Grace came down from the stage not expecting anyone to say anything to her.

"That was one hell of an audition, I must say," Levi said loudly as he walked over to her. She quickly looked away, not wanting to appear overly confident. She blushed when she saw Winston coming up behind Levi with a grin from ear to ear showing those pearly whites.

Winston spoke next. "Well, I thought I'd seen the best, but this was…"

Wait a minute; she wasn't auditioning for Winston anyway, she was auditioning for Levi. She loved to dance and he wanted to see what she could do. Now it was up to him.

After a few minutes of nobody else saying a word, she turned to head back to the dressing room to change. Suddenly Maxi grabbed her arm. "Wait just a minute, Grace." She tried to pull away but Maxi's grip was too tight. "So, Levi, do we have a new dancer or what?"

He didn't answer. He just stood there staring at Grace like she was an alien. "Go on home and we'll talk about it later," Levi said coolly as he downed the last of his drink.

Grace was upset, but she didn't want to show it. She had proven her point to Levi. Sugarbaby and the other dancers followed her to the back room.

"Girl, where did you learn to dance like that?" Sugarbaby asked. Looks like she was the chosen spokesperson. They were probably jealous or just tired from their own shift.

"It's just something I picked up along the way." Grace would never tell them she'd danced there before back when Anthony was the owner. It didn't matter anyway. The decision was Levi's, and he was being rude about it. She knew his kind. He wanted to string her along as a waitress, and then use her as a fill in. But Grace was better than just a substitute dancer. She wanted to be the main event, especially on Friday nights.

"Well, I must admit, you are the best dancer I've ever seen," Sugarbaby said. "If Levi doesn't have you up and dancing by next week, he is crazier than I thought. Plus, the money you could bring in this place would put his name right up there with Charlotte's Webb over on Prospect Avenue."

Maxi walked in at the tail of their conversation. "Don't worry; I'll talk to Levi. He's just being stubborn, but you have to know him like I do. He will come around. You'll see."

"Thanks, Maxi, but at this point I want him to make up his own mind. I don't need you to talk to him," Grace said. "He has to know if he wants me to dance or not dance." Grace was busy changing into her street clothes. She was ready to go home. She had made her point. Now it was up to him.

It was almost 3:00 a.m. when Grace and Maxi left the club along with the other girls, leaving Candi, Winston, and Levi to close up shop. Tony and Harley walked them to their cars.

As Grace bent over to throw her bag into the back seat, Tony patted her on the behind. She immediately spun around and slapped his face hard. "Don't you ever put your hands on me again!"

He was furious, but he backed away. He called her a few choice names, then retreated back inside the bar. Maxi could not believe he had overstepped the no touching boundaries. "Now, he knows better than that," Maxi said. "Levi needs to check his security cameras. He'll see what he did. That was totally out of line."

Grace was too tired and ready to hit the bed. She rode quietly all the way to the apartment. What in the world was she doing out here anyway, putting herself in harm's way? These were the times when she wanted Hilton to show up and put a man like Tony in his place. He had no business touching her like that. But, who was she fooling? It all went with the territory and she knew it. Did she really expect not to be touched inappropriately in a place like Ace's?

Chapter Ten

——— *e* ———

True to her word, Maxi tried to talk Levi into letting Grace dance. But he ignored her reasoning for another four weeks and did not falter in his decision. Grace was getting dirty looks from the other dancers since that night. Maxi said they thought she was out to take their jobs. The one with the stage name, Honeybun, purposely bumped into Grace as she was waiting tables on a busy Friday night. But Grace didn't care. She just went on about her duties as if it never happened. Besides, she didn't think these dancers wanted to go there with her. She could take her talents elsewhere.

A month later, on a Wednesday night before the club opened up, Grace and Maxi arrived a little early. Grace took advantage of the empty room and walked up onto the stage. No, she wasn't going to dance. It just felt good being up there. She felt comfortable on stage. It was second nature to her.

Suddenly she heard a female voice shouting at her: "Get off our stage. We are getting ready to practice what we professionals get paid to do," the female voice said. Grace wasn't sure whom the voice belonged to but she could almost bet it was Honeybun.

Grace walked down from the stage and said, "No problem." But, before she walked away she heard one of them say something under her breath. None of them expected her to say anything back, so they were shocked when she turned around and as loud as she could, she belted out, "So this is Levi's perception of a professional dancer? Now that is hilarious." She began laughing as she walked away. She knew she was a better dancer than any of these girls and they knew it too.

———————

It was finally closing time. Maxi and Grace were about to leave when Levi summoned Grace to his office. "Levi wants to see you for a few minutes," Harley said. She went to the back and was about to knock on the door when it opened. Levi was standing alone in his office and invited her in. "Hello, Grace. Come on in."

"Hi," she said. She couldn't think of what he had to talk to her about, and if he said anything about her slapping Tony, she was not going to bite her tongue. "You wanted to see me?" Levi closed the door and sat down.

"Yes. Have a seat," he said. "I've been thinking a lot about that dance you did, you and Maxi, and I must say nobody here can pull off a routine like that. I mean, I really liked it—a lot," he said. She remained silent to see where he was going with this.

"And, as you probably know, Maxi's been bugging me to let you dance. So, here's your chance. We're having a private birthday party up in the VIP Lounge on Friday night. I was wondering if you could dance this coming Friday?"

Was he crazy? Her first time dancing at the club, and he wanted to throw her to the wolves immediately in VIP? "But, why can't I dance down here on the main floor, for my first time at least?"

"Well, for one thing, it's going to be jam-packed in here and most of our special guests will be up in VIP, which is where most of the money will be, if you get my drift. Now, it will be a great opportunity for you to make a lot of money that night."

"And, what kind of money are we talking about?" She knew no matter how much she made, Levi would take his cut, which was normal practice for all the dancers.

"At least a thousand to fifteen-hundred dollars. Maybe even more if you do that same exotic routine you did with Maxi." He took a long gulp from his drink. "And I really enjoyed that inverted pole split thing you did."

What! She almost laughed. So he had actually paid attention to her routine. Had he noticed her newest trick—the bow and arrow position upright on the pole? That was her favorite. "So, let me get this straight: you want me to dance upstairs this coming Friday for the birthday party

88

crowd, and you agree to let Maxi dance as my sexy prop on stage with me?"

"Yep. Can you do that for me?"

She sat back as if she was thinking about it. Of course she wanted to dance, but not upstairs. She remembered how the men had groped all over Sugarbaby and left her feeling violated.

"Okay, I'll do it, but only if you provide extra security at both ends of the stage area. I don't want anybody touching me."

"Okay, I can do that. Anything else you need?" Levi was all smiles and seeing dollar signs.

"Also," Grace continued, "since I have to pay Maxi something for being my prop, can you adjust your cut to leave me more to split with her?"

Levi had to think about her offer. Although he really wanted her to dance, he still had to make his cut; that was how the business operated. "Okay, tell you what," he said. "If you make more than expected that night, I'll take my usual cut. But, if it's less than I expect, I'll take less so you'll have enough to give to Maxi. Is that fair?"

She had no other choice. "Yes, that's fair." She got up to leave, but before opening the door she turned to Levi and asked, "Who's dancing before I go out?"

"Honeybun is scheduled to dance at opening," Levi said.

"No. I'll dance first," Grace said. She waited for his reply. She would not dance behind any of these girls. She was too good for that.

"Okay. You dance first. Anything else?"

She was satisfied and it was a deal. She finally opened the door. "Thanks, Levi. You will not regret this."

"We shall see," Levi said. "Oh, and one last thing… you'll need a stage name—something to fit your performance. "Just think about," he said. " Now get going. It's getting late."

———————

The next day was Thursday. After a quick cup of coffee and a slice of toast, Maxi and Grace headed over to Candi's complex. Grace remembered Candi had invited them to use the exercise equipment whenever they wanted. She needed to brush up on her strength training with hand weights and do a few pull and push ups in order to pull off the ultimate dance routine she was planning.

When they arrived at Candi's place, she buzzed them up and handed them frosted glasses of Cosmopolitan as soon as they walked through the door. Five minutes later they were back on the elevator and headed downstairs with the pass code key to the gym. Grace was already in her workout clothes while Candi and Maxi relaxed in the chairs sporting white Capri pants and halter tops. They both looked out of place with straw hats and sunglasses on as if they were going to the beach.

After Maxi and Candi saw how powerfully Grace could move her body, graceful and deliberate when she twisted into various positions, positions neither one of them could ever imagine doing, it didn't take long to brainstorm her stage name—*GRAVITY*, because of her ability to appear to levitate in mid air on that pole.

Grace didn't see anything wrong with using her own name, after all, her style was graceful and her ability to exude a story of emotion through her pole dance routine was amazing. She always tried to demonstrate a passionate and alluring dance routine. Maxi and Candi said because she was able to invert and levitate before spinning around the pole over and over, which took years of practice to get those tricks down to a fluid motion and an amazingly beautiful almost breathtaking work of art, Grace became '*Gravity*' overnight.

Chapter Eleven

ℯ

Friday night came fast. Prior to opening that night someone had decorated the lounge with balloons, happy birthday signs, and confetti throughout the club. There were birthday center pieces on each of the tables with a lighted candle. Crêpe paper ribbon was strung along the mirror behind the bar and around the DJ booth. Jimmy Jazz had a variety of music already blasting out of the speakers. He had a great line up for tonight: Hip Hop, Rap, Reggae, Cuban, Rock and Smooth Jazz. They all worked together to get the people out on the dance floor.

Grace and Maxi were a little anxious. They'd gone through their routine several times back at the apartment and knew exactly what to do. Upstairs in VIP it was decorated with colorful strobe lights focused on the stage area, ready for the festivities. They waited in the back room until the place was filled up. Finally, Winston knocked on their door. "It's time, ladies."

They waited to be introduced. She could hear the

men who jammed the VIP lounge. The place was a circus and Levi was going to get his money's worth tonight. Closing her eyes, Grace thought about Hilton. She knew what she was doing was wrong for a woman of her status. Married with children. She felt a pang of shame run through her until she heard Winston's voice. He was already on the stage enticing the men. She could almost smell their lust, and in a few minutes she would face it with the birthday boy.

Men would be undressing her with their eyes, imagining whatever they wanted to do to her if they had a chance. Nope, that would never happen. She had resolved in her mind that she would never be that desperate.

Grace surprised herself by saying a silent prayer. *God, if You're real, please send my husband to get me out of this place. I don't belong here.* But she knew that wasn't going to happen if it depended on her prayers. She held on to her unbelief in Hilton's God and mocked him every time he prayed for her.

"Coming to the stage now, everybody give it up for Gra-vi-ty. The whole place went wild as they took the stage wearing sexy gothic costumes. Maxi took her seat in the chair off to the side as the music started. Grace moved seductively around the chair as she tied Maxi's hands with the black rope and blinded-folded her with the ribbon—all done to the beat of the music. She then sashayed over to the pole and began her routine.

She pretty much repeated the same routine when she first auditioned for Levi, but added a few new positions for special effect, and for more drama, she changed into a blonde wig with long false eyelashes. Tonight, she wanted the birthday boy to be pleased with her performance.

She immediately slid up the pole into the aerial invert and out to a full split; her armpits held her with a backward spiral spin around the pole; then she pulled off the boomerang—another one of her favorites. The crowd went wild.

It was at this point Grace walked over to Maxi and untied the rope from her wrist giving her three slashes with the rope as if forcing her into submission, before moving seductively around the back of her chair and untying the blind fold. Only this time Maxi stood up and kissed Grace on the lips before slithering down to the floor and crawling over to the pole. Together they did a double butterfly around the pole, then Grace did another split as she slid down the pole to the floor.

Maxi exited the stage as Grace did a belly crawl and snaked her way up to the edge of the stage where a crowd of men were pressing up against the edges throwing money on the stage. She was pleased to see the security guards doing their jobs. She spotted the birthday boy, Antwon Robinson, who played basketball for Cleveland. Most of the men in the room were either ball players or part of their entourage.

He stood in the center with a smile on his lips from ear to ear. Grace bent over and gave him an opened mouth kiss on his lips ending with tracing his lips with her wet tongue.

The crowd went wild. She knew he was pleased with her performance.

As she leaned in again for a final birthday kiss on the cheek this time, he handed her a slip of paper which she quickly tucked inside her bra as she slithered across the floor on her knees back to the center of the pole. She did a final split sliding down the pole letting her bottom bounce on the floor a few times before returning to a split position on the pole, legs wide open until she was finally standing and exited the stage.

The men cheered, clapped, whistled, and chanted, "GRA-VI-TY, GRA-VI-TY." Her name roared through the club. She was sure they could hear her name chanted all the way downstairs. She doubted if Honeybun wanted to follow her performance after that.

Money was everywhere on the stage. Both guards gathered it up as fast as they could and brought it back to Grace and Maxi's dressing room. She could not believe her eyes; there was so much money. She knew for sure Levi would be taking his normal cut of her earnings, but it was all worth it.

Before they had finished changing into their regular clothes, Levi was at their door. He was smiling from ear to ear. Winston was right behind him. "Gravity, I believe you've proven yourself tonight. You are definitely the best dancer I have ever seen by far," he said smiling.

"Why, thank you, Levi. I'm glad you approve."

"Approve! I absolutely loved it. It was more than I expected, and that thing you do with Maxi." He turned to Maxi. "You guys are a great team. Did you see the crowd going wild?"

"Yes, they definitely went crazy when you kissed Antwon," Maxi said. "I'm just glad security was present up front and they barely kept them from rushing the stage."

"Well, I'm just glad our birthday boy is happy." Levi said. "He was raving about you after you left the stage. As a matter of fact, he's waiting on you out on the floor. He wants to meet you both and buy you a drink."

"Okay, cool. Tell him we're on our way," Grace said.

Levi walked over to the table where Maxi was still counting all the money and placing it in stacks. "It's all there. Count it for yourself!" Maxi said.

He did, and afterwards he took his cut and handed her the rest. There was still a lot of money left. She and Maxi were going to go shopping that weekend for sure. "This is all yours. You girls deserved it," Levi said. "Now hurry up and get out on the floor. Don't want to keep a celeb waiting too long."

Grace pulled out the note Antwon had passed to her on stage. *Can we meet later?* She didn't want to read any more into it other than that he wanted to buy her a drink. Grace could never put aside the fact that she was a married woman with children. It had been a little more than four months now and she missed her family. But, nothing felt as satisfying and gratifying as dancing on stage and all the cheers, the attention, and love she felt from others after her routine. Whatever it was she received from dancing didn't matter at this point. She just loved it.

Fifteen minutes later they were out on the floor. Tony was headed in her direction with Antwon and another ballplayer. She didn't know his name, but she recognized him. "Gravity, this is Antwon. Antwon, meet the lovely Gravity." Tony turned to Maxi. "Oh, and this is her friend, Maxi." Maxi ignored Tony trying to get one in and focused on this handsome eye candy standing next to her. This just might be Mr. Right!

"Hello, ladies. Can I get you something from the bar?" They placed their orders with the waitress and claimed the seats on the leather couch. Maxi was preoccupied with one of Antwon's friends, while Levi stood across the room and observed every move they made.

The room had cleared out somewhat. Honeybun was up dancing, but most of the patrons were scattered or had gone downstairs already. Levi finally realized allowing Grace to dance first was the best decision after all. Some patrons had left the club and gone on to the next, doing what they call "the bar crawl." Maxi said that was when they went from bar to bar, staying a half hour at each one.

Levi sat across the room staring at Grace and Antwon. His mind was racing a mile a minute. In all the months he'd owned Ace's Lounge he'd never taken in that much money in one night. None of the other dancers made anything even close to what Grace (Or was it Gravity?) brought in that night. Whatever it was, she was the best of the best. He knew if he put her in the line up every Friday night, he would be a millionaire sooner than later.

Now, all he had to do was convince Grace and Maxi to do that routine every Friday night. No more waiting tables for Grace. With the tips she made, that would put him over the top. He would be in the big league like Charlotte's Webb Lounge, a well known club in the area. His thoughts were running wild. He had already surpassed his attendance over that hole in the wall a few blocks down—the Velvet Dog, although the Velvet Dog was known in Cleveland for becoming the go-to club for any drug you desired. Coke, meth, Quaalude, weed, pills—you name it, you could easily buy it at the Velvet Dog. They were obviously paying the cops big bucks under the table to look the other way.

Levi made a mental note to get the marquee changed out front. Something big and bright like those movie theater marquee lights. And he'd include her name in big letters; *"Featuring GRAVITY."* People would see his club on a whole new level. And allowing Antwon to have his birthday party at the club was a good PR move. The word would get out to the other ball players. He couldn't help but laugh as he watched her have fun talking with a huge celebrity.

Grace went back to the apartment with Maxi that night counting out her money and her blessings. She was suddenly reminded of a song her boys would sing during Vacation Bible School: *Count your blessings, name them one by one, count your many blessings, see what God has done.* The sudden recollection of the old church hymn dragged her demeanor down. Grace was the first to admit, she had never been a hard core Christian, but she believed just enough. She had said her fair share of prayers, not to mention the scores of bargains she'd made with God to get her out of a jam. She did not always hold up her end of the deal when God came through. But, she was pretty sure, right now, God was upset with her big time.

Chapter Twelve

— *et* —

Over the next few months, Grace danced at Ace's Lounge and the money was flowing freely. Occasionally, she changed her routine. Sometimes her routine called for changing her costume and Maxi was enjoying being a tiny part of it. Being a part of spreading the wealth around was exuberating. Even Candi and Jeffrey were quite surprised how things had changed at Ace's since Grace and Maxi had partnered up. Levi was at the top of his game in the city. For every home game in Cleveland, the ball players would find the time for a little fun at Ace's Lounge. During the playoff games the place was jammed to the point where the Fire Marshall had to stop anyone else from entering the establishment for their own safety.

It didn't take long for Grace to learn to distinguish the window shoppers from the spenders; those who were browsing, just out looking, from those who were eager to part with their cash for a little fun, maybe even a little one-on-one attention.

At some point, Grace had agreed to give private dances for some of Levi's personal friends, but not before they'd worked out the financial agreement and what his cut would be. Still, she made a big profit with every client.

One day as she was getting dressed to go into work, Grace thought about the most recent private session with one of Levi's influential friends—a city councilman. She always referred to him as 'The Councilman.' She didn't want to know his real name—ever. That would be getting too familiar with her clients and that was a no-no.

The Councilman had booked a room at the Ritz Carlton Hotel in downtown Cleveland. He'd given Levi all the details to pass on to Grace. He gave special instructions and insisted on Grace coming alone for this dance. Levi assured her it was on the up-and-up, but just in case, he sent his bodyguard, Harley, in another car and instructed him to hang out at the hotel and make sure she returned to her car safely. Harley was instructed if he hadn't heard back from Grace by a certain time, he was to come upstairs to check things out.

Grace arrived a little early. She was nervous because this was a big time public figure, a councilman, who had apparently turned his eyes to the underground world that was going on in the city, and was just on the news himself bashing drug pushers, prostitutes, and criminal activities in his ward.

The Ritz Carlton was one of the top establishments as far as hotels in Cleveland. Only the rich and famous could afford to stay there. She stepped into the empty elevator and hit the button for the tenth floor. As the elevator started to move up to his floor, she was startled when suddenly a voice spoke to her softly. She turned to look around, her eyes darting from corner to corner, from the ceiling to the floor to see if there were any hidden speakers. Nothing. A few minutes later there it was again: "*Grace, get out now!*" Was this a joke? Was somebody playing a trick on her? Was she supposed to retreat back to the lobby and get out now? It didn't make any sense.

She tried to swallow but her throat was dry. The elevator door opened to the tenth floor and she stepped out. The carpeting was plush and beautiful. There were gold framed mirrors strategically placed along the walls and lined up between doors down the corridor. The furniture looked like each piece cost a million dollars. Very expensive and elegant. Grace adjusted her skirt in one of the mirrors and walked toward the room number he'd given to her.

She knocked twice before the Councilman opened the door and welcomed her inside. It was supposed to be a private dance with just the two of them, but to her surprise there were four other men inside the room.

Grace looked at the Councilman sideways, puzzled. He knew she wasn't expecting anyone else. "Don't worry, they won't hurt you. They're just here for a little fun, and to observe. That's all. But if you want them to leave I will be happy to throw them out."

The Councilman looked at the men and winked. Grace walked past them to check things out. At first she thought about walking out and heading straight to Ace's to let Levi know what was going on down there. But then, she thought about the extra money she could make for herself and keep it with no cuts to Levi.

After walking around the suite she finally turned to the Councilman. He was afraid she would leave so he held the door open.

"Okay, I'll do it but it will cost you a hundred dollars extra," she said.

The Councilman was pleasantly surprised. He let the door go and it closed on its own.

"Oh, that's no problem." He dug into his pockets and pulled out a wad of bills. He peeled off five twenties and handed them to her, grinning like a Cheshire cat from ear to ear.

Grace put her hands on her hips and shifted from one leg to another.

"Umm, no-no. I meant a hundred dollars extra from each of you."

"What! But I thought…" The Councilman knew she was serious and knew his friends would be pissed at him, but they had already made up their minds to stay and had given their wives excuses for being out so late that night, so why not. They gave in and pulled out their cash money. One of them threw his twenties across the floor in disgust.

"Come on, man. Don't treat the lady like that," the Councilman rebuked. "Now, pick up the cash and hand it to her like a gentleman."

He did as he was told reluctantly, and poured himself another shot of Patron.

Grace counted it all out then stuffed it into her bag. She asked the Councilman to pour her a drink and headed toward the bathroom to change into her costume.

Ten minutes later she walked out. She was dressed in a cowgirl outfit and matching hat with a black long ranger mask, white furry chaps and sparkling silver boots. Underneath all that she wore was a hot pink G-string and pink pom-poms taped to her skin at the tips of her breast. The rest of her skin was covered with shiny, sparkly oils.

Immediately, all eyes snapped forward when she whirled across the floor. The men sat up in their chairs positioned in a circle around the suite. They stared slack-jawed at her as she started her performance for them.

She moved across the floor twisting and doing gyrations—swaying in one fluid motion, hips flowing in perfect sync to the music she had on repeat playing from her iPhone. The men begin to get louder as she gyrated to the edge of the Councilman's seat. She knew this was his private session so she gave him the most attention, but not too much. She was taught to only give them a little at a time. Keep them hungry and coming back for more.

She did a mini lap dance for him before gripping the front of her belt that fastened the chaps, and with one movement she ripped them completely off leaving her in only the cowboy boots, the hat, the long ranger mask and hot pink G-string with pink pom-poms. Her half naked body glistened and sparkled with sweat and glitter oil. She knew how to make a lasting impression.

She flipped her body over toward the center of the floor and came down slowly into a full split in front of the fat guy who was salivating at the mouth. She thought he was going to choke on his own saliva. She bounced a few times while in the split position then hopped up off the floor and spun around waving her cowboy hat at the men. She sure hoped the Councilman was a man of his word, because these men were getting antsy and about ready to burst out of their pants and grab her. The one guy who was pissed that he had to pay money was sitting on the edge of his seat about to burst open. No telling what they all would do to her if things got out of hand.

Back on her feet, her hands laced behind her neck, her body curving like a snake and swaying to and fro as she worked her way over to the edge of the bed where she positioned herself in the center of the bed in several positions until the music was almost over. One of the men tried to grab her leg, but she slipped away courtesy of the glitter oil—a little trick the dancers used to prevent the men from getting a secure hold on them.

When the song came to a second ending she stood up. The men clapped and whistled. The Councilman stood up to allow her to move away from the vultures. Oh, yeah, they wanted her badly. She was grateful the Councilman made good on his word and didn't allow these strangers to touch her.

She finally removed the mask revealing her beautiful face and tossed it towards the Councilman. He caught it and put it up to his nose to drink in her fragrance before tucking it into his pocket. She grabbed her cell phone from the table and hurried into the bathroom to change back into her regular clothes. She leaned heavily against the narrow counter before the mirror, her heart beating so fast she could hardly breathe.

And there was that voice again: *"Grace, why are you doing this?"* She looked around, but she knew she was alone. It was just her imagination or perhaps her self-conscience talking to her. Guilt needled at her heart and she tried to shove it away; wallowing in guilt did no one any good. She knew doing these private dances was not right. There was a big difference working at Ace's Lounge and doing a private dance in hotels. This was her very first time dancing for more than one man at a time, she was not prepared for the rush of adrenaline it produced. It scared her. It was times like this she wished Hilton would burst through the doors and rescue her from this place.

When she walked out the bathroom the men blew kisses to her as she passed them and she blew kisses back at them. She and Maxi had taught each other a lot about dancing. It was their job to lead their imagination of what could be in their fantasy world to keep them coming back for more.

"You okay?" the Councilman asked as she stood in the foyer with all five of the men staring at her with hungry eyes.

"Yes, I'm good," she said.

"Oh, you were more than good," one of the men blurted out.

"Well, looks like you scored a nice chunk of cash for yourself," the Councilman said with a bit of sarcasm in his voice.

"Yes, and thank y'all very much," she said loud for the others to hear as she headed toward the door.

It was then she realized she could keep doing this behind Levi's back and he would never know. She didn't need the money, but it was the excitement of it all, the adrenalin and rush it gave her.

The Councilman thanked her for coming and promised this was not the last time he would need her services. The other men were drinking themselves into a stupor before they had to return home to their wives and explain why they had sweated out their suits.

She met Harley in the lobby of the hotel and he escorted her to her car.

"So, how was it dancing for that Councilman?"

"Oh, it was alright. In and out—and it was over."

"He didn't touch you did he?"

"Oh, no, he knows the rules. Levi wouldn't stand for that."

"Well, good. Glad to hear. If you hadn't come down when you did, I was headed up there for you. You were ten minutes late."

"Well, I'm glad you didn't come up there. It all worked out now, didn't it?"

Grace was careful not to mention that the Councilman had four other men in the room, and how she'd danced for them all and made a quick five hundred bucks for herself. That was not including the cut she'd receive from what was already paid to Levi for setting her up with the Councilman. She knew the big bucks were in the private dances for these big time guys, and she'd only danced for thirty minutes. No, she was not about to let him or Maxi in on her little secret.

Many Months Later

HOSEA 3:1-3

You would think love would have its limits. I do not think anyone would have looked down on Hosea for bailing out on his marriage at this point. Yet, the Lord had Hosea to stay in the marriage. He wouldn't let him go free. Why? Hosea was to be a picture of God's amazing love and faithfulness to a group of people who often did not return God's faithfulness.

Even when God's people turn their backs on Him and run to the world to indulge their pleasure, God's love doesn't quit. He doesn't give up. He doesn't look for an out. He still pursues us. How can we even begin to describe a love that is so deep that we would pursue an adulteress in spite of. And yet this is exactly what God told Hosea to do:

"The Lord said to (Hosea), 'Go show your love to your wife again, though she is loved by another and is an adulteress. Love her as the Lord loves Israel, though they turn to other gods and have loved the sacred raisin cakes.'

Chapter Thirteen

————— ❧ —————

Hilton never ceased praying and fasting for his wife while she was gone. Plenty of times he had tried to reason with God: why would she place a life in the world over her covenant vows as a wife and mother to him and their three children? Still, he loved her more than ever before and continued to cover her with prayer for God's divine protection.

His constant prayer was: *"Why do you have me to love her so deeply, yet she prefers the love of the streets."* God was always consistent in His answer.

Not long after their wedding, Hilton had purchased a modest Tudor style home in the suburbs of Pennsylvania, and after that, the children started coming. Grace had taken charge of redecorating it into a beautiful home. She never had to work outside of the home. Hilton provided more than enough money for his family. They never lacked for anything.

God had to continually remind Hilton of his

specific prayers when he'd prayed and asked God to bring him a wife. He dreamed of how beautiful she would look, how sweet she would smell, how lovely her hair would be. He remembered so well the day God had answered that prayer and he'd met his wife, Grace.

———————

At the age of seventeen, Hilton had decided to finally get serious about becoming a Christian and had spent the rest of his teenage years single. He'd only dated in small groups with others from the church. He thought he'd met "the one" after graduation when a young lady from his youth group started calling and talking with him everyday. However, after the summer ended, she left the country with her parents to do missionary work in Zimbabwe, and that was the end of that. Hilton was left alone as he poured his free time into his part time job at the pizza place and took college classes to fill up his time. He finally landed a good job making good money, but in his heart he knew something was missing.

So whenever Hilton prayed, he always asked God to send him a wife. He asked specifically for someone who loved God first and would love him second. He waited patiently until one day he went with the youth group to Cleveland where his pastor was ministering at a revival service. There were a lot of people under the huge tent in the parking lot, but one girl stood up front by herself. She was different. Beautiful. There was a sense of loss in her eyes and she looked to be searching. Her skin was smooth and she had big eyes like a doll. She seemed guarded, yet confident.

Hilton got a chance to meet her after the service was over, and by the end of the night, they had exchanged phone numbers. He wanted to find out more about her. All he could think about was what if she was "the one."

Over the next couple months they talked on the phone and he soon realized what a humble, lovely, and sincere person she was. They could only meet up in person whenever he could drive back to Cleveland on the weekends. But, she also had a job and her weekends were always booked. They worked it out to meet from time to time. But, Hilton continued to pray and ask God if he was wasting his time or if she was "the one"? *Lord, is she the one I should marry? Give me some type of sign.*

The months passed by and he finally met some of her friends, but none of them were believers like he was. They dressed provocatively and stayed out late at nights in clubs and bars. He had no idea what that lifestyle was all about. He knew she was part of their world, but something was different about her. There was one thing he was certain of and that was he was smitten and had fallen in love, and that scared him.

Then one night as he was praying, the Lord said to him clearly, **"Take Grace as your wife."** At first, he didn't receive what the Lord was telling him. Surely a woman from her background had no place in the life of a God-fearing man, a church-going believer like he. He needed a godly wife—one who feared the Lord and was willing to serve Him daily. But God continued to speak to him during his prayer time. So, he prayed even harder because he did not want to make any mistakes. As a Christian, he did not want to make a wrong move; too much was at stake and he didn't want to ruin his witness or have any of his church friends get the wrong idea that he was a backslider. They could see clearly that Grace was a woman of the world and wondered if he really heard God.

Over the next several months, on three different times, he'd asked God again if this was "the one." And all three times God had answered him, yes. But this one particular time God spoke with authority, as if it were a command: **"Hilton, do My will. Take her as your wife**."

After that, he finally got up enough nerve to ask Grace if he could ask her a personal question. But he did not know what to say so he went back home and prayed some more. He tried to sleep without dreaming of her, but it was no use. The next morning it was clear to him what he had to do.

"Lord, you said do your will, and you already know what type of girl I need to be my wife. I've waited for your choice, so if she is the one, please give me the boldness to speak up and please open her heart to hear me through You."

The following weekend when they met to go out to dinner and a movie, he did not know that Grace had also prayed, "Let something happen today between Hilton and me, or take this man out of my heart." She confessed long afterwards that she, too, had strong feelings for Hilton, but she did not know how to express it.

The evening was getting late when he felt a nudge from the Lord to be brave. So before he could change his mind, he asked her, "Grace, do you feel anything for me?" She responded, "Whoa!" Not knowing what that meant, Hilton thought perhaps he should wait for another time. But then he relaxed and began to tell Grace what the Lord had put in his heart and how he felt about her. And she began to tell him of her feelings also. By the end of the evening it was clear to them both that it was more a question of when, not if. And, to make it official, he asked Grace to marry him and she said yes.

"A man that findeth a wife findeth a good thing and obtaineth favor from the Lord" (Proverbs 18:22).

It had been a little over ten months since Grace had left their home on the eve of their fifteenth wedding anniversary dinner. Shane and Christi had a beautiful little baby girl. They'd named her Faith Marie. Her sons were delighted to have a little sister. Between Hilton's mother-in-law and Christi, they were a God-send. Christi had helped out as much as she could with his boys.

Shane couldn't understand for the life of him why Hilton would put up with such foolishness from his wife. They'd witnessed these run-a-way escapades from Grace, and it was beginning to get old. Yet, Hilton always obeyed God and went out, found her, and brought her back home. He loved Grace enough to forgive her and life went on. Only, this time. Shane could see how it was really wearing Hilton down. His spirit was low and he sensed a bout of depression setting in. Each time it took more and more to encourage Hilton to keep going on. "Keep pressing on," he'd told him. They often prayed together for wisdom and strength.

It was during a Sunday evening service at church when Hilton was pouring out his petitions at the altar for his wife and kids, when the Lord spoke to him loud and clear—as He always did: ***"Hilton, Go show your love to your wife again, though she is loved by another and is an adulteress, love her as the Lord God loves her, though she's turned to other gods and loved the world more than her own self."*** *(Hosea 3:1-3)*

Hilton had heard those words before from the Lord, therefore, he didn't question its source. He knew it was time. He didn't waste any time making arrangements with his mother-in-law to keep the kids. He didn't know how long he'd be gone. Sometimes it was a quick turn-a-round. Sometimes it took days to bring her home. Sometimes she came willingly, sometimes not. It was always different depending on the situation.

Hilton had an idea where she might be, but he trusted God to lead him to her. One thing he knew about his Grace, she loved to dance, and had danced before in a club somewhere in downtown Cleveland. It was a chance he had to take. The Lord had spoken to him and he wouldn't turn a deaf ear to His demands.

Hilton set out to find his wife. He arrived in Cleveland late that Friday night and circled around downtown for hours. He drove past the Velvet Dog Lounge, Charlotte's Web, and Ace's Lounge. Grace had danced at all of them over the years, before they were married, and afterwards also. He never understood what drew her into these places. But it was his lot in life to find her and bring her back home—again.

Chapter Fourteen

———— *&* ————

Hilton pulled up in front of Ace's Lounge. A huge marquee was blinking out front over the door arches announcing in bright strobe lights, '*Featuring GRA-VI-TY Tonight.*' Who was Gravity? He decided to find out. If she wasn't there, he'd check the Velvet Dog and then Charlotte's Web. If it got too late he was planning to get a hotel room overnight and start his search again the next night and the next night. Whatever it took, he was not going home without her.

He parked his truck in Ace's lot and walked inside. The place was packed from wall to wall, mostly men. He moved through the crowd trying to blend in, but most of what he saw repulsed him. All he could think to do was to keep looking and praying: *Yea, though I walk through the valley of the shadow of death, I will fear no evil.*

The heavy smell of alcohol was overwhelming, and for those who had to go outside to smoke, they brought the smell back inside in their clothing and hair. He had to pray hard. His goal was to find his wife and then get out of there. He was not going home without her.

Making his second round through the club, there was no sign of Grace anywhere. He checked both bars to see if she was serving. He waited near the bathrooms to see if she would walk out. He stood by the DJ to see if she would pass him on her way to get more drinks. On the dance stage was a tall slender red head. He watched her dance around the pole for a minute. But it was not Grace. Perhaps she was at another club, he reasoned. He did a final scan of the main floor. He noticed someone had remodeled the inside of the club with an upgrade that made it look more metro.

It was no use. She wasn't here, so he decided to check out The Velvet Dog. As he headed toward the front door, he could hear loud chanting coming from the upstairs area. He hadn't even realized there *was* an upstairs to Ace's Lounge. He moved a little closer to the steps and pretended to lean up against the wall where there were crowds of people gathered, some going up and some coming down. He wondered what you had to do to get up there.

"Well, well, well. Hello there, Freddie," a female voice said. He turned around and looked behind him. *Was she talking to me? If so, she had the wrong person. And who was this Freddie person anyway?* "Don't act like you don't know me. *She is talking to me.* You never called me back after I gave you my private phone number. What's up with that, Fred-dee?"

He thought about it then decided to play along with her. Perhaps, this was his ticket to getting upstairs. "Oh, hey.

I'm sorry, but I lost my cell phone and all my numbers were lost with it. Can you give it to me again?" Hilton was playing it cool. He knew this girl was drunk and wasn't seeing too clear. "You know, I thought about you for days after my phone was lost. I really did mean to call you," he said.

"Aw, how sweet. Why don't you come on upstairs and you can buy me a drink if you wanted to see me so badly. I'll give it to you again."

Bingo. He was right behind her heading up the steps. "Okay, that sounds great."

As soon as they reached the top, a security guy looked at her and then at Hilton, from head to foot. He feared they would suspect him as an undercover cop since he was dressed like a geek. He was thinking fast when to his relief, she said, "Oh, he's with me."

Hilton wiped sweat beads from his forehead as they both walked past and into a sea mob of men, most of them gathered around the stage area. He looked closer to see who was dancing and saw two girls on the stage. He needed to get closer since they had on all black gothic type costumes.

His friend grabbed his hand and led him over to a corner bar. "So, what have you been up to, Freddie?" She stumbled then plopped down on a bar stool. He had to admit the stranger was a beautiful specimen. Although he wasn't interested in her, he still had to use her to help him find Grace.

The stranger ordered a glass of Petron for them both. Hilton had no idea what he was about to put up to his lips. It was as clear as water. As soon as he took a small sip, he gagged and wanted to spit it out, but he hid it with a cough so as not to let on. He cleared his throat and held the glass in his hand. "Look, I've been out of town for awhile. My job keeps me traveling, so…" He held a cool steady voice.

"Aw! Well, Freddie, let's make the best of your time here tonight." She threw her head back and laughed, then took a big gulp of her drink. Without making a face she swallowed her drink down as if it was a glass of water.

About the same time Hilton heard the crowd shouting, "Gra-vi-ty! Gra-vi-ty! Gra-vi-ty! Gra-vi-ty," Who in the world was Gravity? Whoever she was, the marquee outside said she was featured tonight. He tried to look closer, but couldn't tell if one of the girls on stage was Grace or someone else, but whoever she was, the crowd loved her.

The crowd was so loud you had to shout to be heard. "I don't get to spend much time partying," he shouted to his lady friend. "But it's nice to be out for a change."

There were plenty of wolf whistles from the men in front of the stage as one of the girls sitting in a chair with her wrist tied up with some type of rope and blindfolded started to gyrate in her chair. The other girl was dressed in a black short cropped halter top that was barely past her belly button. She wore black leather shorts and thigh high tall patent leather stiletto boots. She was wearing a black wig with bangs that stopped just below her eyebrows and the rest was straight and long. With the ruby red lipstick she reminded him of a dominatrix.

He suddenly felt the need to get out of there. But he had to get away from this strange woman before she gave his identity away to security. He had to find out if Grace was even in the building, perhaps in one of those back rooms. There was always a back room in these types of places.

He fidgeted with the ice cubes in his drink. "This is my first time up here," he shouted. "Who are the girls on stage, the one everybody is going crazy over?" He motioned to the stage area toward Gravity.

"Oh, that's one of Levi's newest money makers. Levi scored big paper when she signed on to dance here. She and her friend do this exotic dance routine. Drives all the men crazy. Levi hit the jackpot when he found her. This place hasn't been the same since she arrived."

"Hmm." Hilton wondered for a second. "Can I ask you, is Gravity her real name?" He knew it was a risk to ask such a bold and direct question to this woman, but he knew he'd never see her again after tonight so why waste anymore time in this place if Grace was not even here.

"I have no idea. I don't come up here often myself, but on the few nights I am here, I've only heard them call her Gravity, and they love Gravity. But, enough talk about her. What are we going to do when we leave here tonight?"

Hilton had to think fast. The dancing act was finally over and the stage cleared. For some reason he wouldn't have been shocked at all to find out that the girl under all that long black hair and those patent leather boots was, in fact, his Gracie. He was planning his exit as soon as he heard the clapping and chanting calm down, but first he had to get away from this stranger, so he came up with a plan. "Listen, I need to run to the men's room. Will you wait here for me?"

"Aww, Fred-dee! Where else would I go? I mean, we have a date later on tonight. Right?" In his mind, she was dreaming as well as drunk. He had to make his move now while the crowd was dispersing.

"Yes, sweetheart. We sure do, so don't you go anywhere. Okay?"

"Okay, Freddie. I'll be right here waiting for you, so hurry back now." She threw her head back seductively then took another drink from her glass.

Chapter Fifteen

—————— ᴇᴛ ——————

Hilton made his way across the dark crowded room and down the hall in the direction the barmaid had pointed for the men's room. But instead of going inside, he waited in the hallway until the coast was clear and went further down toward 'the rooms.' He quietly opened the first door he came to. A dancer was getting dressed. "Can I help you?"

"No. No. I'm sorry. I was looking for somebody else." He hurriedly closed the door and moved on to the next door. He listened for a minute as he heard more voices. He slowly opened the door and, surprisingly, there sitting on a plush white bar stool in front of a huge wall-to-wall mirror outlined with theater lights was Gracie. She had pulled her wig off and a few pieces of her costume were already on the floor. It looked as if she had just started to wipe the heavy makeup off her face when she looked up as he opened the door.

Levi and Winston were also inside with the girls counting the money that had been thrown onto the stage. Winston immediately stood up. "Hey, bro? Did you make a wrong turn?" he asked him. But Hilton kept his eyes locked on Grace. She knew that look. It was the look of quiet determination. He was finally here. He came to take her home.

"No, I didn't. As a matter of fact, I made the right turn."

"And, what business do you have back here with these women?" Winston asked getting a lot closer to Hilton. He was trying to intimidate him, but it wasn't going to work.

"I came to take my wife home," he said.

"Your wife?" Winston said in a loud voice. "I'm sorry, buddy, but you must be drunk. Now, I suggest you go back out that door, and get you a glass of seltzer water. Try to sober up or something."

"Oh, I'm not drunk. As a matter of fact, I don't drink. Like I said, I'm here to take my wife home." Hilton whispered a quiet prayer under his breath: *When the evildoers approached me… they themselves stumbled and fell (Psalm 27:1).*

Winston turned toward Maxi and Grace, wondering which of these women was possibly married to this intruder. "And, do you see your wife anywhere in this room?"

"Yes, she's sitting right there." Hilton pointed to Grace. Grace quietly stood up to acknowledge his presence.

"Hilton."

"Hello, Grace. Will you please tell these men the truth?"

She stood and walked over to Hilton. At first he thought she was going to reject him, which could cause things to turn ugly and dangerous. But, thank God she came to her senses.

"I'm sorry, Winston, but yes, what this man says is true. I am his wife and the mother of our three children." She stared at Hilton as if it was too good to be true, yet he could tell she longed to stay in her world.

She inspected Hilton as she would a stranger, looking him up and down. His hair had grayed a little more over time and he was a lot thinner. His eyes had a sadness that was beyond reproach. Her heart broke for him.

Suddenly, Levi spoke up. "Well, well, Grace. You never told us you were married and had children. Now, how do you think I'm supposed to handle this situation? You think I'm going to let you walk out of here just like that? I can't allow you to walk away from me now, Grace. We've invested too much to turn back. I mean, you're our main attraction. You owe me and the club big time if you walk out of here and give all this up."

The whole time Levi spoke Grace was ignoring him. She couldn't take her eyes off Hilton. She wanted him to grab her into his arms and run. But it wasn't that simple. Hilton tore his eyes from Grace and glanced over to the other girl. He recognized her from the last time he came to Cleveland to rescue his wife from this same club. She definitely recognized him also.

Maxi knew this day would come sooner rather than later. She wondered why it took Hilton so long to come get his wife. As soon as she saw him, her heart went out to their children. Countless times she'd ask Grace that million dollar question: Why come here to this hell den and dance for strange men just to take their money? She could never understand women like Grace.

After standing there for what seemed like eternity, Grace finally spoke up. "Hilton, can you leave me to talk with my boss for a few minutes? I just need to explain some things to him."

"No, Grace, I am not going anywhere unless you're with me. I am not leaving this room or this place without you, so you can start talking now."

Grace looked over at Levi and Winston. "He's my husband. My children need me. I have to leave. I have to go with him."

"But what are you saying, Grace? That you are going to walk away from me just like that?" *She had done it before.* "Grace, without you I might as well go out of business. This establishment is nothing without your name on the marquee. Do you hear me, Grace? Nothing." Although Levi was getting nowhere, he continued to plead. "In a matter of months you've put Ace's Lounge on the map. Celebrities from all over the country are starting to come here when they're in town, and they're coming just to see you. Think about it for a minute before you throw all of this away. Football players, basketball players, city officials, and don't forget how generous the councilman had been to you. Some have paid you very well for private dances. Look at how much money you've made in a short period of time."

Grace was surprised Levi knew about her deal with the city councilman and his friends that night, charging them extra. But still, she ignored him. "You can't walk out on me," Levi tried again. "Don't do this, Grace. I will pay you double. Anything you want, but please don't leave."

Grace was in a bad spot. It was always like this—a sticky situation whenever Hilton showed up, and always difficult—far too difficult with each time. The pull of the world wrestled with her conviction to return home to her family. She was torn. She knew Hilton would never give up on her no matter how many times she went back out. She knew he loved her, unconditionally. He had so much love and compassion for her. She had rejected him and walked away to a life of the unthinkable. She never would admit how she and Winston had been intimate a few times in the back room downstairs, but she knew it wouldn't last long. Hilton would always return looking for her, like he did tonight.

Levi was getting agitated and was ready for this conversation to be over with. "No. I am not going to let you walk out on me just like this, Grace. No way. You can tell this man to go back where he's been all this time. You belong to me and you know dancing runs through your veins. You love to dance, Grace. You remember that day you begged me to let you dance? So, look at you now—a star. No way am I going to let you go! So, you listen to me. What is it going to be? I need to know right now."

Grace was surprised herself after listening to Levi how much he'd paid attention to her whereabouts and what she was doing. If she truly needed the money, by now, under any other circumstances, she would have already sold her body. But, Levi had looked out for her, protected her from drugs and the street life some of the other dancers were involved with, although she was one foot away from stepping over the threshold.

Hilton held his ground. He knew he had to prepare to fight for his wife. He was not leaving without her. He had heard the voice of the Lord and he knew what he was doing was the right thing.

"Look, I didn't come to start a fight," Hilton said. "I have come prepared to pay you whatever money you would have made from Grace working for you, but only up to one year's worth. You can take it or leave it, but I am not leaving here without my wife."

Levi knew this man was serious. How could he stop him? She belonged to him. They had children together. He knew if he called the cops, they would arrest him instead. What could he do? If Grace left, it would cost the club a lot of money to stay on top. He would sink back to the bottom and Charlotte's Web would be number one again. He didn't have anybody who could dance like Grace or Gravity. Maybe with Maxi still being here, she could do a routine with one of the other girls. But, who was he fooling. There was nobody who could dance like Grace. She was the absolute best he'd ever seen.

For what seemed like hours, Grace stood there with her eyes locked on Hilton. Such a determined man who knew what he wanted and wouldn't take no for an answer. She felt a stab of pain in her heart for how she'd treated him over the years. Why does she keep doing this? Why does he keep coming back to get her? She wasn't worth it. He deserved a wife who believed like he did, who wouldn't bolt every time things got too stressful. She knew Hilton loved her, and she loved him. But, he would never understand her need to be out there. She'd never disclosed all the things that had happened to her as a little girl—things that made her into the woman she was today. No, he could never understand her.

She knew Hilton was not leaving without her. Things could get ugly so she finally agreed. "Yes, Hilton, I'm coming home with you." Hilton took her into his arms and held her close. She could smell his cologne and his scent. She missed him so much. He smelled her hair, which smelled like drinks and cigarettes, but it didn't matter to him. He had found his wife and was taking her back home.

"Look, I'm a man of my word," Hilton said. He pulled out his wallet and asked Levi how much would it cost to take his wife away from this place? Levi didn't bat an eye naming some outrageous figure. Hilton gladly wrote out the check and handed it to him. It was the total amount of six months of his salary. Hilton smiled as he tore the check from his checkbook and handed it to Levi. His only focus was his wife and it was worth any amount to take her back home with him and their children.

"I hope this check is good. If not, I see your address is on here."

Hilton smiled. "Not to worry. It's good. Now, if you'll excuse me. We need to hit the road."

Levi and Winston hurried out of the room. Neither one turned to say goodbye to Grace. Grace hugged Maxi as they cried together and said their goodbyes. She helped Grace gather her things from the dressing room, and half the money from their performance that night. Maxi told her she would send whatever she had left at the apartment via courier. Mainly boots, shoes, and purses.

Maxi watched as Grace zipped up her Fendi satchel and thought about how she'd never forget her good friend. But, she also hoped she'd never see her again—at least not inside the night club. Maxi knew Grace didn't belong at Ace's Lounge, even though she couldn't deny Grace was the best dancer this side of the Cuyahoga River.

By the time Grace and Hilton left the club, Ace's Lounge had cleared out as it was after closing. Thank God the strange woman he'd met who called him Freddie, was long gone. Hilton and Grace walked arm in arm together down the steps and out the front door. Tony and Harley gave them some kind of look as they walked past them and into the parking lot. Hilton turned to Grace and kissed her on the forehead and said, "It's time to go home, my love."

And with that, they drove out of the lot and out of the city. Neither one turned to look back. After a while she was the first to speak up. "I'm so sorry. Can you please forgive me?" The floodgates of her tears opened up and she was trembling.

Hilton waited until he was back on the freeway before he said a word. Finally, he placed one hand over her hands. "Grace, I will always love you no matter how many times I have to do this. I prayed for you every day you were gone. I missed you so much it hurts, and the children miss you, too."

She cried even harder when Hilton mentioned the children. He patted her hands to let her know everything was going to be alright. "You're with me now and we're going home."

She mopped her face with her blouse sleeve. He handed her tissue from the glove box and she blew her nose. Between sobs she managed to ask, "Hilton, can you please find it in your heart to forgive me? I am such a fool. I am so ashamed."

"Grace, of course I forgive you. The Bible says for me to be forgiven by God, I must forgive those who trespass against me. So, based on His Word, I must forgive you. Forgiveness is not an option, it's a commandment."

Grace was not going to let it go that easy. She didn't understand his God and how forgiveness worked, but she knew if anybody could teach her, Hilton could. After a while, she asked him if he thought his God would forgive her also.

"Oh, my dear Gracie, God will forgive anyone who asks Him to forgive them. It's very simple. You've heard me talk about being born again many times. It's as simple as that. God loves you, Grace, in spite of yourself. He waits patiently for His dear sons and daughters to come to Him for forgiveness. He is always ready to hear the sound of your voice praying the 'sinner's prayer.'"

Grace had heard Hilton pray with many of their friends and family. The times she did attend his church, he had led many souls to salvation. She wanted to be saved from herself, but she needed Hilton to be by her side to help her understand. She couldn't explain it, but for some reason, her heart was now opened to hear more about his God and what a loving God He was, even to a sinner like her. But, could she forgive herself was the question.

———————

They arrived home sometime in the middle of the night. Hilton ran around the car and opened the door for his wife. She was worn out and tired. The night life had stolen her joy and her strength.

He had already planned out the rest of the evening. No point in getting the boys until the next day. His plans went smoothly. She soaked that old sinful nature off in the hot tub until her skin was raw and wrinkled. Hilton gently dried her off and rubbed Shea butter lotions all over her body, soaking in the new and refreshed layers.

Once she had been treated by his healing hands, he held her hands together and led her through the sinner's prayer for the first time. He knew she was ready to turn her life around. But he also knew there would be more challenges ahead. He was convinced God was teaching him patience and long suffering. But he was up for the challenge.

After she repeated the sinner's prayer and they opened their eyes to each other, for the first time, Grace saw her husband through the eyes of God—broken but solid in his faith—steadfast. She saw the hurt and pain she'd caused and she knew this time she was home for good. "There is no one in this world who means more to me than you do, Hilton." Grace dropped her head as tears began to flow down her cheeks.

Hilton pulled his wife into his arms, holding her tight as he pressed his face against her neck. Her warm tears fell on his cheeks. "Not me, sweetheart. It's not me I want you to love in this whole wide world. I want you to love *Him* more than you do me," Hilton said as he pointed towards the heavens.

Hilton knew that was going to take time and teaching. Grace began to shake as the tears came in like a flood. Her hands came up and covered her face as sobs racked her body. "I'm sorry… I'm so sorry…"

"Don't." Hilton tilted her face up toward him. "Don't apologize to me. I love you and I've missed you … so much. The kids missed you. I wanted to die when you were not here to celebrate both their birthdays. I didn't want to live in a world where I couldn't have you here with me."

Turning towards the end table, Hilton reached for his worn out Bible with the dog-eared pages. He turned to the book of *The Song of Solomon*, his favorite book to read to his wife. He knew she would remember and it would soften her spirit toward God. He flipped through a few pages and began reading as they both lay across the bed. Grace listened intently to his words:

> *I went to my garden and breathed the sweet fragrance. I ate the fruit and honey and I drank the nectar and wine. Celebrate with me. Raise your glasses and let's celebrate— to our life; to our love. Let me in my dear, my beautiful dove; let us consummate our love for each other. For, I am soaked with the dampness of the night and drenched with dew, shivering and cold. Raise your glasses and let us celebrate—To our life! To our love! Oh how I have ravished you in my heart my love, with thine eyes, with the chain of thy neck. How fair is thy love! How much better is thy love than wine! Your love smells of thine ointments that are all spices! Thy lips are as drops of the honeycomb: honey and milk are under thy tongue; and the smell of thy garments is like the smell of Lebanon. Raise your glasses my love. Come let us celebrate—To our life! To our love!*

After he finished, Hilton turned to look at his wife; her eyes were heavy, but locked on him as if they both had heard the voice in the room. She was used to hearing that 'still small voice' by now. That voice had spoken to her on several occasions throughout the time she had been out in the world. Yet, she had never connected it to the voice of God.

He gently whispered into Hilton's ear and reminded him of His Word: *"Hilton, go and show your love to your wife again."* And he pulled her into his arms and did as God had commanded.

Epilogue

So I bought her for fifteen shekels of silver and about a homer and a lethek of barley. Then I told her, "You are to live with me many days, you must not be a prostitute or be intimate with any man, and I will live with you."

And the LORD said to me, "Go again, love this woman who is loved by another man and is an adulteress, even as the LORD loves the children of Israel, though they turn to other gods and love cakes of raisins." So I bought her again for fifteen shekels of silver and a homer and a lethek of barley. And I said to her, "You must dwell as mine for many days. You shall not play the whore, or belong to another man; so will I also be to you."

She's Always a Woman to Me

She can kill with a smile
She can wound with her eyes
She can ruin your faith, with her casual lies;
And she only reveals what she wants you to see
She hides like a child,
But she's always a woman to me.

She can lead you to love
She can take you or leave you
She can ask for the truth
But she'll never believe you;
And she'll take what you give her, as long as it's free
Yeah, she steals like a thief
But she's always a woman to me.

–Billy Joel

How to Rest in God's Grace While God Works in Your Marriage

Difficult issues that linger in your marriage can cause great stress in your relationship over time. It's tempting to work hard to try to bring about the changes you hope to see, but doing so is a futile effort. No matter how hard you try, you can't change your spouse or improve your marriage on your own. The good news is that your marriage *can* change for the better when you entrust it to God and start relating to your spouse as God relates to you—**with Grace**.

When you base your marriage on grace, you can let go of the burden of trying to change it yourself and rest in the confidence that God will work *through you* to bring about change. Here's how:

Entrust your spouse to God. As long as you're trying to change your spouse on your own, you're sabotaging your goal because you're interfering with the work God wants to do in your spouse's life. Your spouse may not be able to hear

God's voice if your own voice is drowning His out. So give up working toward your own plans for your spouse, and instead, focus your energy on praying for God to work in your spouse's life in whatever ways are best. Trust God to do what you can't do to help your spouse. By getting out of the way, you'll invite God to work more in your spouse's life and help your spouse notice God more.

Ask God to redeem your past mistakes. Don't waste time or energy regretting bad decisions you've made in the past that you can't do anything to change now, such as marrying an unbeliever (for example). Move forward by praying for God to redeem your mistakes, despite the consequences you've suffered, so that good purposes will ultimately come out of the bad situations in your marriage. Continue to pray for the Holy Spirit to give your spouse greater faith as she/he seeks God.

Look to God—not your spouse—to validate you. Don't base your sense of self-worth on how your spouse responds to you (which is bound to be unreliable), but on how God responds to you. As a sinful human being in a fallen world, your spouse may fail to express himself or herself to you in ways that affirm your value; but God will never let you down. Ask the Holy Spirit to help you see yourself as God sees you. **Keep in mind that your value doesn't depend on your spouse's opinion of you, but on your Creator's**

complete love for you. Derive confidence from God's love. When your spouse sees confidence in you, your confidence will command his respect.

Rely on Jesus to give you what your spouse can't. When your spouse neglects you or fails you (as they're bound to do sometimes, since she/he is not perfect), forgive your spouse and turn to Jesus to meet your needs. Whenever you feel lonely, ask Jesus to help you sense the reality of His constant, loving presence with you.

Shift your focus from external behavior to internal transformation. Rather than focusing on how religiously your spouse behaves (such as how often she/he attends church, reads his/her Bible or prays at home, or how much time and money they give to others in need), focus your main concern on the state of their soul. While religious activities are noble in that they accomplish good purposes, a man or woman doesn't have to look religious to be a godly spouse. Stop pressuring your spouse to fit into a certain template of what you think a good Christian spouse should look like. **Accept your spouse just as they are and decide to love them unconditionally, as God does.** When your spouse experiences your unconditional love, she/he will stop being as defensive as they may has been about spiritual matters with you, and will be inspired to draw closer to the source of unconditional love: God.

Confront your spouse about mistreatment and abuse.
You do not have to tolerate cruel words or controlling behavior from your spouse. Protect yourself (and your children) from abuse of any kind. Speak calmly and firmly to your spouse about the problem, refusing to be drawn into an argument, and informing him/her of clear consequences you will enforce if they disrespects you in the future. Then be sure to follow through with those consequences from leaving the room **to leaving the marriage temporarily through a separation if that's what's necessary for her/ him to take you seriously** and pursue the healing he needs to truly change. Rely on the Holy Spirit to give you courage and to empower you throughout the process. Remember, physical abuse is never acceptable and is against the law.

Improve communication between you and your spouse.
Seek to understand your spouse better by listening carefully to him/her when they talk and asking them to tell you what they thinks they hear you say in discussions so you can clarify if necessary. When you're frustrated by an issue in your marriage, talk *to* your spouse rather than *about* him/her to others. Address problems with your spouse's behavior, but don't attack his/her character. Make your goal understanding each other better, rather than winning arguments.

Let go of unnecessary stress by simplifying your schedule. Keeping too busy can cause tension in your marriage, which you can avoid by eliminating some activities. Ask God to show you which of your activities aren't truly important in light of what has eternal value, then delete those activities from your schedule so you can focus on what matters most—your marriage.

For more information on Marriage Workshops or Seminars, log onto our website at:
http://brokenwingsministry.org

Discussion Questions

1. Why did the Lord say to Hosea, "Go and marry a prostitute and have children with her"? (Hosea 1:2-3 and also 3:1-3)

2. How does this passage parallel with today's rebellious people? Explain.

3. What are some of the devices that drive people back into the world? (Hosea 2:5-7)

4. What were the names of Hosea and Gomer's three children? Why were these names given to them? (Hosea 1:4-9)

5. Why does God allow people to do their 'own' thing? (Hosea 4:1-6)

6. Sometimes we have to hit _____ _____ and then maybe he'll come looking for me. (Hosea 5:15, Message Bible)

7. "O Israel, come back! Return to your God!" Just like Hosea, what price did our God pay to redeem us from our sins? (Hosea 14:1)

8. Following God's path will always get you to where you want to go. Explain. (Hosea 14:1-9, Message Bible)

9. Do you know of anyone in your past or present in whom you can see 'Gomer' struggling? How can we lead them back to the cross? Explain.

10. How does forgiveness work in the life of the believer? Why do we sometimes struggle with forgiving ourselves?

11. How would you describe God's love for Grace, even while she was not walking upright?

12. The Bible says, 'All things work together for the good of them who are called according to His purpose.' How does this relate to Hilton and his faith that God would bring his wife back home?

Other Books by the Authors

- *Is it Worth the Wait? (Is it possible to reclaim your virginity again)*
- *You Did it Grandma, You Did it! (Children's Book)*
- *When Leslie Left (When loves goes brutally wrong)*
- *Finding God on Mapquest (The Long Road Home)*
- *While You're Waiting (What to do while you're waiting on God)*
- *Black River Junction (A story of Tragedy, Love and Forgiveness)*
- *Coming Soon ~ Toxic Love~ (Marriage Behind Prison Walls)*

Authors can be contacted at:

E-mail: brokenwingsministry@yahoo.com

Website: http://jenniferrankins.com

www.ingramcontent.com/pod-product-compliance
Lightning Source LLC
Chambersburg PA
CBHW060353090426
42734CB00011B/2125